Latin Phrases & Quotations

Revised Edition

Also by Richard A. Branyon . . .

Treasury of Roman Love Poems, Quotations & Proverbs

Richard A. Branyon, editor and translator

This collection of love poetry includes works in the original Latin with side-by-side English translation. Here are love poems 12 notable Roman poets, including Catullus, Virgil, Horace, Ovid, and Juvenal, along with numerous proverbs and quotations about love. With its simultaneous Latin and English text, this book is a perfect classroom tool or study aid for students of Latin who want to practice translations on their own.

127 pages • 5 x 7 • 0-7818-0309-8 • $11.95 hardcover • (348)

Treasury of French Love Poems, Quotations & Proverbs

Richard A. Branyon, editor and translator

This collection of French love poems, quotations and proverbs reflects a culture deeply affected by the affairs of the heart. Subjects such as lust, betrayal, true love, marriage and obsession are explored in 25 poems and over 100 proverbs and quotations. The text includes the original French with side-by-side English translations. Also available on audiocassette read by professional actors and native speakers.

127 pages • 5 x 7 • 0-7818-0307-1 • $11.95 hardcover • (344)
Audiobook: 120 minutes • 0-7818-0359-4 • $12.95 • (580)

All prices subject to change. **To purchase Hippocrene Books** contact your local bookstore, call (718) 454-2366, or write to: HIPPOCRENE BOOKS, 171 Madison Avenue, New York, NY 10016. Please enclose check or money order, adding $5.00 shipping (UPS) for the first book and $.50 for each additional book.

Latin Phrases & Quotations

Revised Edition

Richard A. Branyon

HIPPOCRENE BOOKS
New York

Dedicated to the memory of my mother
Roberta Mahaffey Branyon
who taught me the value of an education

Copyright © 1994, 1997 by Hippocrene Books, Inc.
Second printing, 1999.
All Rights Reserved.

For information, address:
HIPPOCRENE BOOKS
171 Madison Avenue
New York, NY 10016

Library of Congress Cataloging-in-Publication Data

Branyon, Richard A.
Latin phrases & quotations / Richard A. Branyon. — Rev. ed.
p. cm.
ISBN 0-7818-0260-1
1. Latin language—Dictionaries—English. 2. Latin language-
-Terms and phrases. 3. Quotations, Latin. I. Title.
PA2365.E5B73   1997   96-38535
473'.21—dc20   CIP

Printed in the United States of America

CONTENTS

FOREWORD

Even after some two years now, I still remember the surprise and pleasure I felt upon first examining Richard Branyon's Dictionary of Latin Phrases and Quotations. Here was a true "reader's companion," I realized, to have at the ready when reading—or even carefully re-reading—so many works of literature belonging to the Western tradition from Classical Roman Antiquity down to our own time. Not only professors, teachers, and students outside the field of Latin studies but for that matter anyone with a Liberal Arts background would surely find this resource to be helpful and of remarkably practical usefulness. In addition to explaining words and phrases that might be wholly unfamiliar and otherwise undecipherable to a reader with a limited knowledge of the Latin language, this guide also performs the valuable service of making clear many other expressions whose meaning might otherwise remain imperfectly understood or even unintentionally misinterpreted—something I have found happening to myself all too frequently in the past.

But now, armed with this compact and eminently usable reference tool, I have realized that encounters with unfamiliar Latin words and phrases in my general reading no longer need to be disconcerting or frustrating experiences. Thanks to Richard Branyon's book, our reading can proceed without breaking stride on such occasions. I admire what he has done and can recommend it with enthusiasm to anyone seeking such a ready-reference tool when undertaking the reading of material likely to contain Latin words and phrases without accompanying translation or explanation.

FREDERICK W. VOGLER

Professor of French,
University of North
Carolina at Chapel Hill
Department of Romance
Languages
November, 1993

PREFACE TO THE FIRST EDITION

During the past five years, colleges and universities in the United States have witnessed a resurgence of interest in the liberal arts and humanities. For almost two decades, colleges and universities saw their enrollments increase in fields of business, engineering, science, and related diciplines, while enrollments in the liberal arts often suffered declines. This may have been acceptable for a while. Certainly, the education of men and women in these fields is important in order to maintain a competitive stance in our international economy. However, as students of those disciplines have grown older, many have experienced regret in not having taken more courses in liberal arts while they were in college. Although many of today's graduates have had some exposure to a foreign language, very few have had any significant exposure to classical literature or to the classical languages, Latin and Greek.

This dictionary has been compiled to supplement this hiatus in classical knowledge. Although it certainly does not purport to serve as a substitute for the study of Latin, this dictionary can help the reader attain a higher level of appreciation for our classical heritage and lead to an improved understanding of many of the great works of literature. This dictionary serves as a bridge between the normal desk dictionary which may contain 200 to 300 Latin expressions and a standard Latin dictionary which contains only single-word entries.

The entries in this dictionary have been selected from the great literary works of Western civilization and from references containing the most commonly encountered foreign language expressions. The reader should note that *every single expression* in this dictionary has appeared in some literary work in the English language, often without a direct translation. In other words, the author had expected the educated reader to understand these expressions without further explanation. Of course, this is an unwarranted assumption when one realizes that a majority of the literate public has never had any significant exposure to Latin and that most readers experience difficulty upon encountering these foreign expressions without translation.

These entries were selected according to their relative importance in the great literary tradition of Western thought and according to their relative frequency in literature and articles appearing in periodicals. Expressions and phrases which are used only within the confines of a single discipline, such as medicine and law, have been avoided for the most part. Only those expressions which have appeared in books and articles intended for the general public have been included. Also, very few single-word entries have been included, because the more common Latin words which have been assimilated into English can be found in any good desk dictionary.

Another point of which the reader should be aware is related to the print style used in the presentation of foreign expressions. In general, foreign expressions are shown in *italics* in a printed book, or by means of underlining in a typed manuscript. However, a few of the more commonly used expressions have been completely assimilated into English language during the past century and require no italics. Should the reader be concerned about the appropriate print style for any specific expression, he or she should consult a recent dictionary such as *Webster's New World Dictionary*, third edition, or the *Random House College Dictionary*, second edition.

The reader should also note that the Latin alphabet consisted of only twenty letters, most of which were quite similar in style to their counterparts in modern English. The Latin alphabet of classical antiquity did not include the modern K, J, W, X, Y, or Z. I have strictly adhered to the conventional spelling of all Latin words and phrases which originated in the classical period. However, during the Middle Ages and Renaissance, a time when many of the great classical works were rediscovered and translated into other languages, a few changes occurred in the Latin alphabet. Many scribes began to use the modern "J" in words which had previously been spelled with "I" and these words received the pronunciation of a soft "g." Common words affected include "ius" (the etymon for justice), which became "jus," and "iuria" (the etymon for jurisdiction), which became "juria." For those expressions which originated *after* the Renaissance and appear in literature *only* with the modern spelling, I have presented with the "J." For all other expressions I have retained the classical spelling, using the "I." For the purpose of this reference work there were no phrases or quotations which began with the modern "J," therefore; the reader will not find a separate "J" section in the main body of the dictionary.

A

ab absurdo	from the absurd
ab abusu ad usum non valet consequentia	consequences of abuse do not apply to general use
ab actu ad posse valet illatio	from the past one can infer the future
ab aeterno	from the beginning of time
ab asino lanam	wool from an ass; blood from a stone
a bene placito	at pleasure
abest	he or she is absent
abeunt studia in mores	pursuits change into habits (Ovid)
ab extra	from the outside
abiit ad majores	he or she has gone to the ancestors (died)
abiit ad plures	he or she has gone to the majority (died)
abiit, excessit, evasit, erupit	he has departed, gone off, escaped, broken (Cicero)
ab imo pectore	from the bottom of the heart
ab inconvenienti	from the inconvenience involved
ab incunabulis	from infancy; from the cradle
ab initio	from the beginning

LATIN PHRASES AND QUOTATIONS

ab intra	from within
ab invito	against the will; unwillingly
ab Iove principium	from Jove is my beginning (Virgil)
ab irato	from the angry man; unfair
abnormis sapiens	a natural born philosopher (Horace)
ab origine	from the origin; from the first
a bove majori discit arare minor	from the older ox the younger learns to plow
ab ovo	from the egg; from the beginning
ab ovo usque ad mala	from the egg to the apples; from beginning to end
abscissio infiniti	cutting off an infinite part
absens haeres non erit	the absent one will not be heir
absente febre	without fever
absentem laedit cum ebrio qui litigat	to quarrel with a drunk is to wrong a man who isn't even there
absente reo	the defendant being absent
absit invidia	may ill will be absent; no offense intended
absit omen	may the omen be absent; God forbid
absolvo	I absolve; I acquit
absque	without; but for
absque hoc	but for this; apart from this
absque ulla nota	without any marks

ab uno ad omnes	from one to all
ab umo disce omnes	from one example, learn all (Virgil)
ab urbe condita (A.U.C.)	from the foundation of the city (753 B.C., reference to Rome)
abusus non tollit usum	abuse of a right does not invalidate use
abyssus abyssum invocat	hell calls upon hell (the Vulgate)
a capite ad calcem	from head to heel; entirely or completely
accedas ad curiam	you may approach the court
accessit	he or she came near; a runner-up
accipiunt leges, populus quibus legibus ex lex	they consent to laws which place people beyond the pale of the law
accusare nemo se debit, nisi coram Deo	no one is bound to accuse himself, unless before God
acerbus et ingens	fierce and mighty
ac etiam	and also
Acheruntis pabulum	food for Acheron; food for the gallows
a caelo usque ad centrum	from the sky to the center of the earth
a cruce salus	salvation (comes) from the Cross
acta eruditorum	contributions to a cause
acta est fabula	the drama has been acted out (Augustus)
acta sanctorum	deeds of the saints (Jean Bolland)

actio ex delicto	cause of action; reason for a lawsuit
actio personalis moritur cum persona	personal action dies with the person
actum agere	to do what has already been done
actum est	it is all over
actum est de republica	it is all over with the commonwealth
actum ne agas	do not redo that which has been done
actus curiae	act of the court
actus Dei	act of God
actus reus	the criminal act or the guilty act
a cuspide corona	from the spear a crown
ad absurdum	to the absurd
ad alium diem	at another day
ad amussim	according to a rule; accurately
ad aperturam libri	at the opening of a book
ad arbitrium	at will; at pleasure
ad astra	to the stars; to the ultimate ends
ad astra per aspera	to the stars through difficulties (motto of Kansas)
a dato	from the date
ad baculum	to the rod; appeal to force, not reason
ad augusta per angusta	to honor through difficulites
ad calendas Graecas	to the Greek calends; never
ad captandum	for the sake of pleasing

ad captandum vulgus	appealing to the emotions of the crowd
ad clerum	to the clergy
ad crumenam	to the purse; appealing to self-interest
ad damnum	to the damages; amount demanded
addendum	something to be addded
adde parvum parvo magnus acervus erit	add a little to a little and there will be a great heap (Ovid)
additur	let it be increased
ad effectum	until effectual
a Deo et rege	from God and the king
adeo in teneris consuescere multum est	imperative to form habits in the early years (Virgil)
a Deo lux nostra	our light comes from God
adesse	to be present
Adeste Fideles	O come, all ye faithful
ad eundem gradum	to the same degree; equal blame or praise
ad extra	to the outside
ad extremum	to the extreme; to the end
ad fidem	to faith; in allegiance
ad filum aquae	to the center of the stream
ad filum viae	to the center of the road
ad finem	to the end; at the end of the page
ad finem fidelis	faithful to the end
ad gloriam	for the glory
ad gustum	to one's taste
ad hanc vocem	to this word

adhibenda est in jocando moderatio	one should employ restraint in his jests (Cicero)
adhibendus	to be administered
ad hoc	to this; for a specific occasion; impromptu
ad hominen	personal attack relating to the individual
adhuc sub judice lis est	the case is still before the court
ad hunc locum	at this place
ad idem	to the same point
a die	from that day
ad ignorantium	to ignorance (of the facts of an argument)
ad infinitum	without an end; to infinity; without limit
ad initium	at the beginning
ad instar	after the fashion of
ad instar omnium	in the likeness of all
ad interim	in the meantime; for the time being
ad internecionem	to extermination
ad invidiam	to envy or prejudice
ad judicium	to judgment or common sense
adjuvante Deo labor proficit	with God's help, work prospers
ad libitum (ad lib)	at pleasure; extemporaneously or freely
ad limina apostolorum	to the thresholds of the Apostles
ad litem	for the specific lawsuit

ad litteram	to the letter; in a precise manner
ad locum	at the place, at a specific location
ad majorem Dei gloriam	to the greater glory of God (motto of the Jesuits)
ad manum	at hand; ready and prepared
ad meliora vertamur	let us turn to better things
ad misericordiam	to pity; appealing to mercy
ad modum	in the manner of
ad multos annos	after many years
ad nauseam	to the point of sickness or disgust
ad nocendum patentes sumus	we all have power to do harm (Seneca)
ad partes dolentes	to the painful parts
ad patres	to the fathers; dead
ad paucos dies	for a few days
ad perpetuam rei memoriam	for the perpetual remembrance of the thing
ad personam	to the person; relating to the individual
ad populum	to the people
ad praesens ova cras pullis sunt meliora ad quem ad quod	eggs today are better than chickens tomorrow
ad quem	to or for whom; to or for which
ad quod	to which; for which
ad quod damnum	to what damage

ad referendum	for reference; for further consideration
ad rem	to the thing; relevant to the present matter
ad saturatum	to saturation
adscriptus glebae	a person bound to the soil; a serf
ad sectam	at the lawsuit of
adstante febre	when fever is present
adsum	I am present; to be present
ad summam	in short; in a word
ad summum	to the highest point
adulter	corrupter; seducer
ad unguem	to the fingernail; with great precision
ad unguem factus	a highly polished work; to perfection
ad unguem factus homo	a man polished to the nail (Horace)
ad unum omnes	all to one; in a unanimous fashion
ad usum	according to custom
ad usum Delphini	for the Dauphin's use; expurgated
ad usum externum	for external use
ad utrumque paratus	ready for any event; prepared for the worst
ad valorem	according to value
ad verbum	to the word; verbatim
ad verecundiam	appeal to modesty in an argument
adversa	things having been noted
adversa virtute repello	I repel adversity by valor

adversaria	that which has been turned to; commentary
adversus	against; contrary to
adversus bonos mores	against good morals
adversus solem ne loquitor	don't speak against the sum; an obvious fact
ad vitam	for life; for the duration of a person's life
ad vitam aeternam	for eternal life; for all time
ad vitam aut culpam	for life or until a misdeed
ad vivum	to the life
advocatus diaboli	devil's advocate
aedificatum	that which is built
aeger	to be sick; medical excuse of a British student
aeger amore	love's sickness
aegra amans	lover's sickness
aegrescit medendo	the disease worsens with treatment (Virgil)
aegri somnia vana	a sick man's dream; hallucination (Virgil)
aegrotat	he is sick; certificate denoting illness
aequabiliter et diligenter	uniformly and diligently
aequales	equal parts
aequam servare mentem	to preserve a calm mind; equanimity (Horace)
aequam memento rebus in arduis servare mentem	remember to maintain a calm mind while doing difficult tasks (Virgil)
aequanimiter	with composure; with equanimity

aequilibrium indifferentiae	state of exact balance between two actions
aequitas sequitur legem	equity follows the law
aequo animo	with a calm mind; with equanimity
aequo pulsat pede	(pale Death) knocks with equal foot (Horace)
aere perennius	more durable than bronze; everlasting
aes alienum	money belonging to another; a debt
aes triplex	triple brass; a strong defense
aestimatio capitis	estimation of the head; price of a man
aetatis	at the age of
aetatis suae	in the year of one's life
aeternum servans sub pectore vulnus	nursing an everlasting wound within the breast (Virgil)
aeternum vale	farewell forever
affinitas	relationship by marriage
afflatus	breath; breeze; poetic inspiration
afflatus montium	mountain air
afflavit Deus et dissipantur	God sent forth His breath and they were scattered (reference to the Spanish Armada)
a fortiori	with even stronger reason; all the more
a fronte praecipitium a tergo lupi	a precipice in front and wolves behind
age quod agis	do what you are doing; pay attention
aggrediente febre	when the fever increases

agita	shake or stir
agita ante sumendum	shake before taking
agnosco veteris vestigia flammae	I feel once more the scars of the old flame (Virgil)
Agnus Dei	the Lamb of God (portion of Catholic Mass)
a latere	from the side; with confidence
albae gallinae filius	son of a white hen; auspicious event
albo lapillo notare diem	to mark the day with a white stone
albus	white
albus liber	white book
alea jacta est	the die is cast (Julius Caesar, crosses the Rubicon 49 B.C.)
Alere flammam	to feed the flames (Ovid)
alias	otherwise; at another time
alias dictus	an assumed name; also known as
alia tendanda via est	another way must be tried
alibi	elsewhere
alieni appetens	eager for another's property
alieni appetens sui profusus	covetous of another's possession, lavish of his own (Sallust)
alieni generis	of a different class
alieni juris	subject to another law
alienum est onme quicquid optando evenit	what we obtain by asking is not really ours

alimenta	means of support; food, clothing, shelter
alio intuitu	from another point of view
aliquando bonus dormitat Homerus	sometimes even good Homer sleeps
aliquant	an uneven part of the whole
aliquid	something; somewhat
aliquis in omnibus, nullus in singulis	a somebody in general, nobody in particular
aliquot	an even part of the whole
alis volat propriis	she flies by her own wings (motto of Oregon)
alitur vitium vivitque tegendo	vice is nourished by being concealed
aliunde	from another source; from the outside
alma mater	bounteous mother; protective institution
alter	another person; personality of another
altercatio	forensic argumentation; cross-examination
alter ego	one's second self; very close friend
alter ego est amicus	a friend is another self
alter idem	another thing similar in all respects
alter ipse amicus	a friend is a second self
alteri sic tibi	do unto another as to yourself
alternis diebus	every other day
alternis horis	every other hour
alternis noctibus	every other night

alterum alterius auxilio eget	one thing needs the help of another
alterum non laedere	not to injure others
alterum tantum	as much again; twice as much
altiora peto	I seek higher things
altissima quaeque flumina minimo sono labiuntur	the deepest rivers flow with the least sound; still waters run deep
amabit sapiens, cupient caeteri	wise men love, others are mere lechers
amans iratus multa mentitur sibi	an angry lover tells himself many lies
amantes sunt amentes	lovers are lunatics (Terence)
amantium irae amoris integratio est	a lover's quarrel renews love (Terence)
amare et saper vix deo conceditur	even a god finds it difficult to love and to be wise at the same time
amari aliquid	something bitter; a touch of bitterness
a maximis ad minima	from the largest to the smallest
ambigendi locus	room for doubt
a mensa et toro	from table and bed; a legal separation
amici probantur rebus adversis	friends are proved by adversity (Cicero)
amicitiae immortales, mortales inimicitias debere esse	our friendships should be immortal, our enmities mortal (Livy)
amicitia semper prodest	friendship is always of benefit
amicitia sine fraude	friendship without deceit

amicus certus in re incerta cernitur	a friend in need is a friend indeed
amicus curiae	friend of the court; impartial spokesman
amicus est tanquam alter idem	a friend is almost a second self
amicus humani generis	a friend of the human race; philanthropist
amicus Plato, sed magis amica veritas	Plato is my friend, but a greater friend is truth
amicus usque ad aras	a friend to the altars; a friend unto death or until religious convictions prevent action
a minori ad maius	from the lesser to the greater
amissum quod nescitur non amittitur	the loss that is unknown is no loss at all (Publius Syrus)
amor animi arbitrio sumitur, non ponitur	we choose to love, we do not choose to cease loving
amor gignit amorem	love begets love
amor habendi	love of possessing
amori finem tempus, non animus facit	time, not the mind, puts an end to love
amoris vulnis idem sanat qui facit	the wounds of love are cured by love itself
amor magnus doctor est	love is a great teacher (St. Augustine)
amor nummi	love of money
amor patriae	love of one's country
amor proximi	love of one's neighbor
amor sceleratus habendi	accursed love of possessing (Ovid)

amor vincit onmia	love conquers all things (Virgil)
amor vincit onmia et nos cedamus amori	love conquers all things and let us yield to love (Virgil)
amoto quaeramus seria ludo	setting games aside, let's get on to serious matters (Horace)
amo ut invenio	I love as I find
ancilla theologiae	the handmaid of theology; philosophy
Angelus Domini	Angel of the Lord (a Morning Prayer)
anguis in herba	a snake in the grass; a hidden danger
angulus ridet	that corner of the earth smiles (Horace)
angulus terrarum	quiet corner of the world; place of repose
aniles fabulae	old wives' tales
anima	mind, soul, inner spirit
anima bruta	the brute soul
anima divina	the divine soul
anima humana	the human soul
anima in amicis una	one mind among friends
animal bipes implume	a two-legged animal without feathers (Plato's definition of a human being)
animal disputans	an argumentative person
animal rationale	a reasoning person
anima mundi	the power governing the physical universe
anni nubiles	marriageable years

animis opibusque parati	prepared in minds and resources (a motto of South Carolina)
animo et facto	in intention and fact
animo et fide	by courage and faith
animo non astutia	by courage, not by craft
animum pictura pascit inani	with the vain picture he feeds his soul (Virgil)
animus capiendi	with the intention of taking
animus et prudentia	courage and discretion
animus furandi	with the intention of stealing
animus meminisse horret	my soul shudders at the recollection (Virgil)
animus non deficit aequus	equanimity does not fail us
animus revocandi	with intention of revoking a contract
anno	in the year of
anno aetatis suae	in the year of his or her age
anno Christi	in the year of Christ
anno Domini (A.D.)	in the year of our lord
anno Hegirae (A.H.)	in the year of Hegira (622 A.D.)
anno humanae salutis	in the year of man's redemption
annonae caritas	the cost of living is high (Cicero)
anno mundi (A.M.)	in the year of the world's creation (according to Ussher in 4004 B.C., to the Hebrews in 3761 B.C.)

anno regni	in the year of the reign of a specific monarch
anno salutis	in the year of redemption
annos vixit	he or she lived (so many) years
anno urbis conditae (A.U.C.)	in the year of the founding of Rome (753 B.C.)
annuit coeptis	(God) has favored our undertaking (Virgil) (motto on the Great Seal of the United States)
annulus et baculus	ring and staff
annus	year
annus et dies	a year and a day
annus luctus	year of mourning
annus magnus	the great year (cycle of 26, 000 years)
annus mirabilis	wonderful year or remarkable year
ante barbam doces senes	you teach old men before your beard grows
ante bellum	period before the war (usually refers to the American Civil War)
ante Christum	before Christ
ante cibum	before meals
ante diem	before the day
ante litem notam	before commencing litigation
ante lucem	before daybreak
ante meridiem (A.M.)	before noon; in the morning
ante mortem	before death

ante omnia	before all things
ante partum	before childbirth
ante res	before things
ante tubam trepidat	he trembles before the trumpet sounds (Virgil)
apage Satanas	get thee away, Satan
a parte ante	from the part before
a parte post	from the part after
aperte mala cum est mulier, tum demum est bona	only when a woman is openly bad is she really good
aperto vivere voto	to live with unconcealed desire (Persius)
apertum factum	an overt action
apices litigandi	fine points of litigation
apologia	speech made in one's self-defense
apologia pro vita sua	defense of his way of life (Cardinal Newman)
a posse ad esse	from the possible to the actual
a posteriori	inductive reasoning; from effect to cause
apparatus belli	equipment and munitions for war
apparatus criticus	supplementary scholarly information
apparent rari nantes in gurgite vasto	scattered here and there, they are seen swimming in the seething waters (Virgil)
appetitius rationi pareat	let your desires be governed by reason
applicatio est vitae regula	application is the rule of life

a primo	from the first
a principio	from the beginning
a priori	deductive reasoning; from cause to effect
apud	according to; in the writings of
aqua	water
aqua bulliens	boiling water
aqua caelestis	celestial water
aqua calida	warm water
aqua destillata	distilled water
aqua dulcis	sweet water
aqua et igni interdictus	forbidden water and fire (Cicero)
aquae manalis	hand-washing vessel
aqua fervens	hot water
aqua fontana	spring water
aqua fortis	strong water; nitric acid
aqua frigida	cold water
aqua marina	green water
aqua mirabilis	wonderful water
aqua profunda est quieta	still waters run deep
aqua pura	distilled water
aqua regia	royal water; nitric and hydrochloric acid
aqua tofana	water of Tofana; a secret poison
aqua vitae	water of life; whiskey or brandy
aquila non capit muscas	an eagle does not catch flies
a quo	from which
Arata Pentelici	Plowshares of Pentelicus (Ruskin)

arbiter bibendi	the judge of drinking; a toastmaster
arbiter elegantiae	judge of elegance; dictator of fashion
arbitrio suo	on his or her own authority
arbor consanguinitatis	a family tree
arbor vitae	tree of life
Arcades ambo	Arcadians both; two of a kind (Virgil)
arcana caelestia	heavenly secrets
arcana imperii	state secrets
arcanum arcanorum	secret of secrets
ardentia verba	burning words
arena sine ealce	sand without lime; incoherent speech
argentum album	virgin silver; uncoined silver bullion
argentum Dei	God's silver; money given as a bond
argilla quidvis imitaberis uda	you may easily model anything with soft clay
arguendo	to put in clear light; hypothetical situation
argumenta contra	the arguments against
argumenti causa	for the sake of argument
argumentum ab auctoritate	argument derived from authority
argumentum ab inconvenientia	argument based on inconvenience
argumentum ad absurdum	appeal to the absurdity of one's view
argumentum ad baculum	argument appealing to force or threat

argumentum ad captandum	appeal arousing emotions of the crowd
argumentum ad crumenam	argument appealing to self-interest
argumentum ad hominem	argument based on a vindictive attack
argumetnum ad ignorantium	argument based on the opponent's ignorance
argumentum ad indvidium	argument appealing to a person's prejudices
argumentum ad invidiam	argument appealing to an undesirable human trait
argumentum ad iudicium	argument appealing to judgment or common sense
argumentum ad misericordiam	argument appealing to emotions of pity
argumentum ad populum	argument appealing to the popular crowd
argumentum ad rem	argument relevant to the issue; pertinent
argumentum ad verecundiam	argument appealing to venerable authority
argumentum a fortiori	argument for all the stronger reason
argumentum baculinum	argument appealing to physical force
argumentum ex concesso	argument based on concession of opponent
argumentum ex silentio	argument based on lack of firm evidence
arma accipere	to receive arms; to be made a knight
arma dare	to give arms; the accolade of a knight

arma pacis fulcra	arms are the props of peace
armata vis	power having arms; the armed forces
arma tuentur pacem	arms maintain peace
arma virumque cano	of arms and the man I sing (Virgil)
arrectus auribus	with ears pricked up; on the alert (Virgil)
ars amandi	the art of loving
Ars Amatoria	the Art of Love (Ovid)
ars artium	the art of arts; logic
ars artium onmium conservatrix	the art perserving all arts; printing
ars combinatoria	art of combining simple things into complex
ars est celare artem	true pupose of art is to conceal art (Ovid)
ars gratia artis	art for art's sake (MGM trademark)
ars longa, vita brevis	art is long, life is short (Seneca)
ars magna	the great art
ars moriendi	the art of dying
Ars Poetica	the Art of Poetry (Horace)
ars Punica	Punic art, battle tactics
arte magistra	with art the mistress (Virgil)
arte perire sua	to perish by one's own designs
artes honorabit	he will adorn the arts
artes perditae	the lost arts
artes, scientia, veritas	art, science, truth (motto of the University of Michigan)

Artium Baccalaureus	the Bachelor of Arts degree
Artium Magister	the Master of Arts degree
asinus ad lyram	an ass at the lyre; awkward and unfit
asinus asino, et sus sui pulcher	an ass is beautifil to an ass and a pig is beautiful to a pig
asinus asinum fricat	the ass rubs the ass
Asperges	thou shalt sprinkle (Psalm 7)
assignatus utitur iure auctoris	the assignee is possessed of the rights to the principal
assumpsit	he promised; he undertook the contract
astra castra, numen lumen	the stars are my camp, the Deity is my light
Astrea Redux	Astrea Returned (poem by Dryden)
a teneris annis	from the tender years
atra cura	black care
attentat	he or she attempts
at spes non francta	but hope is not broken
atque inter silvas Academi quaerere verum	seek truth in the garden of Academus (Horace)
auctor ignotus	an unknown author
auctor pretiosa facit	the giver makes the gift precious (Ovid)
audaces fortuna iuvat	fortune favors the bold
audaciter et sincere	boldly and frankly
audax et celer	bold and swift
audemus jura nostra defendere	we dare to defend our rights (Alabama motto)

audendo magnus tegitur timor	boldness can mask great fear (Lucan)
audentes fortuna iuvat	fortune favors the brave (Virgil)
aude sapere	dare to be wise
audi alteram partem	hear the other side of the issue
audiatur et altera pars	let the other side also be heard
audita querela	writ giving one leave to appeal
Augustana Confessio	The Agustine Confession
aura popularis	popular breeze; temporary favorite (Cicero)
aurea aetas	the golden age
aurea mediocritas	moderation in all things; golden mean (Horace)
aurea rumpunt tecta quietam	golden palaces disturb one's rest (Seneca)
aureo hamo piscari	to fish with a golden hook
auribus teneo lupum	I have a wolf by the ears (Terence)
auri namque fames parto fit maior	the hunger for gold grows greater as more gold is acquired
auri sacra fames	the accursed desire for gold (Virgil)
auro quaeque ianua panditur	a golden key opens any door
aurora australis	the Southern Lights
aurora borealis	the Northern Lights
aurora musis amica est	the dawn is a friend of the Muses

auspicium melioris aevi	an omen of a better time (motto of the Order of St. Michael and St. George)
aut amat aut odit mulier, nihil est tertium	a woman either loves or hates, nothing in between
aut bibat aut abeat	either drink or depart
aut Caesar aut nihil	either Caesar or nothing
aut Caesar aut nullus	either Caesar or nobody
aut disce aut discede	either learn or leave (motto of Winchester College)
aut insanit homo aut versus facit	the man is either mad or he is composing verses (Horace)
aut mors aut victoria	either death or victory
aut non tentaris, aut perfice	either don't attempt it, or carry it through to the end (Ovid)
aut viam inveniam aut faciam	I will either find a way or make one
aut vincere aut mori	either to conquer or to die
auxilium ab alto	help from on high
auxilium non leve vultus habet	a good face is a good recommendation (Ovid)
ave atque vale	hail and farewell (Catullus)
ave Caesar, morituri te salutamus	hail Caesar, those who are about to die salute you
ave Maria	Hail Mary (song of the Annunciation)
a verbis ad verbera	from words to blows
Ave Regina Caelorum	Hail, the Queen of Heaven

avia Pieridum loca   the Muses' lonely haunts (Lucretius)

avi mala   a bad omen; an unfavorable sign

avi memorantur avorum   my ancestors call to mind their ancestors

a vinculo matrimonii   from the bond of matrimony

avi sinistra   a bad omen; an unfavorable sign

B

balneum	bath
Bancus Communium Placitorum	Court of Common Pleas
Bancus Regis	King's Bench
banni nuptiarum	the banns of matrimony
barbae tenus sapientes	men wise as far as the beard; sciolistic
basis virtutum constantia	constancy is the foundation of virtues
beatae memoriae	of blessed memory
Beata Maria	Blessed Mary (the Virgin Mary)
Beata Virgo Maria	Blessed Virgin Mary
beati pacifici	blessed are the peacemakers (Beatitudes)
beati pauperes spiritu	blessed are the poor in spirit (Beatitudes)
beati possidentes	blessed are those who possess (legal doctrine)
Beatitudes	pronouncements from the Sermon on the Mount
beatus	a blessed person
bella detesta matribus	wars, the horror of mothers (Horace)
bella horrida bella	wars, horrid wars (Virgil)

bellum domesticum	strife among family members
bellum internecinum	internecine war; war of extermination
bellum letale	lethal war, deadly war
bellum omnium in omnes	a war of all against all
bene	well
bene decessit	he has left (died) well; a natural death
Benedicite	invocation of blessing; a prayer canticle
benedictus qui venit	blessed is he who comes (in the Lord's name)
bene esse	well-being
bene est tentare	it is well to try
bene exeat	let him or her go forth; of good character
beneficium	kindness of favor; a benefice
beneficium accipere libertatem est vendere	to accept a favor is to sell one's freedom
bene merenti	success to those who deserve it
bene meritus	having well deserved
bene orasse est bene studuisse	to have prayed well is to have pursued well
bene qui latuit bene vixit	he who has lived in obscurity has lived well
bene vale	a good farewell
bene vale vobis	may you prosper
benigno numine	by the favor of the heavens (Horace)
bibamus, moriendum est	let us drink, for we must die (Seneca)

bibere venenum in auro	to drink poison from a golden cup
biblia pauperum	books of the poor
billa vera	true bill
Biographia Literaria	Literary Biography (Coleridge)
bis	twice; to be repeated
bis dat qui cito dat	he gives twice who gives quickly
bis in die	twice a day
bis in nocte	twice a night
bis in septem diebus	twice in seven days; twice a week
bis peccare in bello non licet	it is not permitted to blunder twice in war
bis pueri senes	old men are twice children
bis repetita placent	the things that please are those repeated
bis vincit qui se vincit in victoria	he conquers himself in victory (Publius Syrus)
bis vivit qui bene vivit	he lives twice who lives well
blandae mendacia linguae	the lies of a flattering tongue
bona	good; property
bonae fidei emptor	purchaser in good faith
bona fide	in good faith, genuine, legitimate
bona fide polliceor	I promise in good faith (Cicero)
bona fides	good faith; documents proving identity
bona gratia	in all kindness
bona fiscalia	public property

bonae memoriae	of happy memory
bona mobilia	moveable property
bona notabilia	noteworthy things
bona peritura	perishable goods
bona vacantia	unclaimed property
bonis avibus	under favorable signs; auspicious
bonis nocet quisqus malis perpercit	whoever spares the bad injures the good (Publius Syrus)
bonis quod bene fit haud perit	whatever is done for good men is never done in vain (Plautus)
bono vinci satius est quam almo more iniuriam vincere	a good man would rather suffer defeat than defeat another by foul means (Sallust)
bonum omen	a good omen
bonum per se	good in itself
bonum publicum	the public good
bonum vinum laetificat cor hominis	good wine gladdens a person's heart
bos in lingua	an ox on the tongue; a heavy silence
brevi manu	with a short hand; in a perfunctory manner
brevis esse laboro, obscurus fio	in trying to become concise, I become obscure (Horace)
brevis ipsa vita est sed malis fit longior	life is short but misfortunes make it longer
brutum fulmen	harmless thunderbolt; vain and empty threat

C

cacoethes	irresistible urge; strong propensity
cacoethes carpendi	a compulsive habit for finding fault
cacoethes loquendi	a bad habit for compulsive talking
cacoethes scribendi	a bad habit for compulsive writing
cadit quaestio	the question falls; the issue collapses
caeca invidia est	envy is blind (Livy)
caelitus mihi vires	my strength is from heaven
caeli enarrant gloriam Dei	the heavens display the glory of God (Psalms)
caelum non animum mutant qui mare currunt	those who cross the sea change only their climate, not their minds (Horace)
calendae	calends; the first day of the month in the ancient Roman calendar
callida junctura	skillful joining; careful workmanship (Horace)
camera lucida	bright chamber; projection device using prism
camera obscura	a darkened room; device to project an image

Camera Stellata	the Star Chamber, renowned court of 16th-century England
Campus Martius	the Field of Mars (assembly ground in Rome)
candida Pax	white-robed Peace (Ovid)
candor dat viribus alas	sincerity gives wings to strength
cane peius et angue	worse than a dog or snake
canis in praesepi	a dog in the manger
Canis Major	the larger dog; constellation of the dog star, Sirius
Canis Minor	the lesser dog; constellation near Orion
cantabit vacuus coram latrone viator	the poor wayfarer will sing in the presence of travelers (Juvenal)
Cantate Domino	sing unto the Lord (Psalm 98)
cantilenam eandem canis	you are singing the same old song (Terence)
cantillatio	the chanting portions of the Catholic Mass
cantoris	to be sung by the precentor (antiphonal song)
cantus firmus	fixed song; Gregorian melody
cantus planus	plainsong; Gregorian chant
capias ad audiendum	writ ordering appearance in court

capias ad respondendum	writ ordering the arrest of a person
capias ad satisfaciendum	writ ordering satisfaction of an order
capiat qui capere possit	let him take it who is able
captantes capti sumus	we catchers have been caught
captatio benevolentiae	reaching after favor
captus nidore culinae	caught by the aroma of the kitchen (Juvenal)
caput inter nubilia condo	I hide my head among the clouds (Virgil)
caput lupinum	the wolf's head; an outlaw or renegade
caput mortuum	worthless residue remaining after a process
caput mundi	the head (or capital) of the world; Rome
caret initio et fine	it lacks a beginning and an end
carmen figuratum	verse printed in the shape of an object
carmen solutum	a prose poem
carmen triumphale	a triumphal song
carpe diem	seize the day; enjoy the moment (Horace)
carpe diem, quam minimum credula postero	enjoy today, trusting little in tomorrow (Horace)
carpent tua poma nepotes	your descendants will pluck your fruit
carpere et colligere	to pluck and to gather
cassetur billa	let the bill be terminated
casis tutissima virtus	virtue is the safest helmet

castigat ridendo mores	one corrects customs by laughing at them
casus belli	reason for war; grounds for a dispute
casus conscientiae	case of conscience
casus foederis	reason for leading to a dispute under a treaty
casus omissus	situation not covered by existing law
casus urbis Troianae	the fall of the city of Troy
causa	cause; precipitating factor
causa causans	cause that causes all things
causa causata	cause resulting from a previous cause
causa efficiens	efficient or effective cause
causa essendi	cause of being
causa fiendi	cause of becoming
causa finalis	final cause
causa formalis	formal cause
causa latet, vis est notissima	the cause is hidden, but its force is very well known (Ovid)
causa mali	cause of evil
causa materialis	material cause
causa mortis	cause of death; in anticipation of death
causa movens	reason for undertaking a particular action
causa proxima	immediate cause
causa remota	remote cause
causa secunda	secondary cause
causa sine qua non	fundamental reason; necessary condition
causa sui	cause of itself

causa vera	true cause
caveant consules	consuls (of the Roman Senate) beware
caveant consules ne quid detrimenti respublica capiat	beware consuls that the commonwealth is not harmed
caveat	let one beware; take caution
caveat actor	let the doer beware
caveat emptor	let the buyer beware
caveat venditor	let the seller beware
caveat viator	let the traveler beware
cave canem	beware of the dog
cavendo tutus	safe by taking heed
cave ne cadas	take care that you do not fall
cave quid dicis, quando, et cui	beware of what you say, when, and to whom
cedant arma togae	let arms yield to the toga (motto of Wyoming)
cede Deo	submit to God
celari vult sua furta Venus	Venus desires her thefts to be concealed
celeritas et veritas	promptness and truth
Cena Domini	the Lord's Supper
censor morum	a censor of morals
certamina divitiarum	struggles of the riches (Horace)
certiorari	to be informed by an appellate review ocurt
certum est quia impossible est	it is certain because it is impossible (Tertullian)
certum voto pete finem	set a definite limit to your desire (Horace)

cessante causa cessat effectus	the cause once removed, the effect disappears
cessio bonorum	the surrender of goods
cetera desunt	the rest are lacking; the text is incomplete
ceteris paribus	other things being equal or remaining the same
characteristica universales	universal characters; ideographs
chartae libertatum	charters of liberties
chorea scriptorum	writer's cramp
Christi crux est mea lux	the Cross of Christ is my light
Christo et Ecclesiae	for Christ and for the Church
cicatrix manet	the scar remains
cineri gloria sera est	glory paid to ashes comes too late (Martial)
cineri gloria sera venit	to the dead fame comes too late
cingulum Veneris	the girdle of Venus
circa (ca.)	about; indicates uncertainty about a date
circuitus verborum	a circuit of words; a circumlocution
circulus in probando	a circle in proof; vicious circle in logic
circulus in definiendo	a circle in definition; vicious circle
circulus vitiosus	a vicious circle; a logical fallacy
cito dispensetur	let it be dispensed quickly
cito enim arescit lacrima, praesertim in alienis malis	a tear is quickly dried when shed for the misfortunes of others

cito maturum, cito putridum	soon ripe, soon rotten
civilitas successit barbarum	civilization succeeds barbarism (motto of Minnesota)
civis Romanus sum	I am a Roman citizen (Cicero)
Civitas Dei	City of God (St. Augustine)
civitas diaboli	city of the devil
clarior e tenebris	(I shine) more brightly from out of darkness
clarum et venerabile nomen	illustrious and venerable name (Lucan)
claves curiae	keys of the court
clavis	a key; a glossary in a text
clerici vagantes	wandering scholars
cochleare magnum	a tablespoonful
cochleare medium	a dessert spoonful
cochleare parvum	a teaspoonful
codex	a volume of manuscripts; a code of laws
Codex Justinianus	the Justinian Code
codex rescriptus	a palimpsest; wooden writing surface
coetus dulce valete	happy meetings, farewell (Catullus)
cogi qui potest nescit mori	he who can be forced has not learned how to die
cogitatonis poenam nemo	no one is punished for his thoughts
cogito, ergo sum	I think, therefore I am (Descartes)
cognati	relations of the mother's side

cognovit actionem	he has acknowledged the action
collectanea	collection of passages from various authors
collegium	members of a group united by common interest
colluvies vitiorum	vile medley of vices; pit of iniquity
collyrium	a medicinal eyewash
colubrem in sinu fovere	to cherish a snake in one's bosom
Columna Bellica	a column of war in ancient Rome
comes iucundus in via pro vehiculo est	a pleasant companion on the road is as good as the carriage (Publius Syrus)
comitas inter communitates	comity of nations
comitas inter gentes	comity between nations
comitia	assembly of the Romans
commisce	mix together
commune bonum	the common good
commune periculum concordiam parit	common danger begets unity
communes loci	commonplace ideas
communibus annis	in common years; the annual average
communi consensu	by common consent
compendia dispendia	shortcuts are roundabout ways
compesce mentem	control your temper (Horace)
complexus	an embracing; aggregate of parts

componere lites	to settle disputes (Horace)
compos mentis	in a sound state of mind
compos sui	master of one's self
compos voti	having obtained one's wishes
compositus	compounded of
concedo	I admit; I concede
concio ad clerum	discourse to the clergy
concordia discors	harmony in discord (Horace)
concursus Dei	concurrent activity of God
condiscipulus	classmate; fellow student
conditio sine qua non	indispensable condition
Congregatio de Propaganda Fide	Congregation for the Propagation of Faith
conjunctis viribus	with united powers
conscia mens recti	conscious of being right (Ovid)
conscientia mille testes	conscience is as good as a thousand witnesses
consensus	by general agreement
consensus audacium	the agreement of rash men; a conspiracy
consensus facit legem	consent makes the law
consensus gentium	unanimity of nations; widespread agreement
consensus omnium	agreement of all members
consequitur quodcunque petit	he attains whatever he attempts
consilio et animis	by wisdom and courage
consilio et prudentia	by wisdom and prudence
consilio manuque	by strategem and manual labor

consilio, non impetu	by deliberation, not impulse
constantia et virtute	by firmness and courage
consuetudo est altera lex	custom is another law
consuetudo pro lege servatur	custom is held as the law
consuetudo quasi altera natura	habit is second nature (Cicero)
consule Planco	in the consulship of Planco; in the good old days (Horace)
consummatum est	it is completed (Christ's words on the cross)
coninuetur remedia	let the medicine be continued
contra bonos mores	contrary to good morals
contradictio in adiecto	contradiction in terms
contra jus commune	against common law
contra formam statuti	against the form of the statute
contra jus gentium	against the law of nations
contra mores	contrary to morals
contra mundum	against the world; an unpopular position
contra naturam	against nature
contra negantem principia non est disputandum	there is no disputing against one who denies the first principles
contra pacem	against the peace
contraria contrariis curantur	opposites are cured by opposites
copia fandi	abundance of talk
copia verborum	abundance of words
coram	before; in the presence of
coram domino rege	before our lord and king

coram judice	in the presence of a judge with jurisdiction
coram nobis	before us; in our presence
coram non judice	before a judge without proper jurisdiction
coram paribus	before equals; before one's peers
coram populo	in the presence of the people
corona lucis	crown of light; a large chandelier
corpora lente augescent cito extinguuntur	bodies grow slowly and die quickly (Tacitus)
cornu copiae	the horn of plenty; abundance
corpus	the body; collection of law or writings
Corpus Christi	feast of the Body of Christ; Holy Eucharist
corpus delicti	body of the crime; objective proof of crime
corpus juris	body of law
Corpus Juris Canonici	body of religious law
Corpus Juris Civilis	body of civil law
corpus omnis Romani juris	compendium of Roman laws
corpus sine pectore	a body without a soul
corpus vile	worthless matter
corrigendum	something to be corrected (pl. **corrigenda**)
corruptio optimi pessima	the corruption of the best is the worst
corruptisima re publica plurimae leges	in the most corrupt state are the most laws (Terence)

cor unum, via una	one heart, one way
cos ingeniorum	a whetstone for the wits
crambe repetita	warmed-over cabbage; stale repetitions
cras	tomorrow
cras credemus, hodie nihil	tomorrow we believe, but not today
cras mane	tomorrow morning
cras mane sumendus	to be taken tomorrow morning
cras mihi	my turn tomorrow
cras nocte	tomorrow night
crassa negligentia	gross negligence; criminal negligence
cras vespere	tomorrow evening
credat Judaeus Apella	let Apella the Jew believe it (I won't) (Horace)
crede Deo	trust in God
credendum	things to be believed; articles of faith
crede quod habes, et habes	believe that you have it, and you do
credite posteri	believe it, future generations (Horace)
Credo	I believe; the Apostles' (Nicene) Creed
credo quia absurdum est	I believe it because it is absurd
credo quia impossible est	I believe it because it is impossible
credo ut intelligam	I believe in order that I may understand (St. Thomas Aquinas)
credula res amore est	love is a credulous thing (Ovid)

crescat scientia, vita excolatur	let knowledge increase, let life be perfected (motto of the University of Chicago)
crescit amornummi quantum ipsa pecunia crescit	the love of money grows as our wealth increases (Juvenal)
crescite et mulitplicamini	increase and multiply (the motto of Maryland)
crescit eundo	it grows as it goes (motto of New Mexico)
crescit sub pondere virtus	virtue grows under oppression
crecitur amor nummi quantum ipsa pecunia crevit	the richer you become the more you love money (Juvenal)
crescentem sequitur cura pecuniam maiorumque fames	as money grows, care follows it and the hunger for more (Virgil)
cribro aquam haurire	to draw water in a sieve
crimen	crime; criminal
crimen falsi	crime of falsification; perjury
crimen innominatum	nameless crime; crime against nature
crimem laesae majestatis	crime of high treason
cruce, dum spiro, fido	while I breathe, I trust the cross
cruce signati	marked with a cross; the Crusaders
crux	cross
crux ansata	a T-shaped cross with loop at top
crux commissa	the tau cross
crux criticorum	the puzzle of the critics

crux decussata	X-shaped cross of St. Andrew or St. Patrick
crux medicorum	the puzzle of doctors
crux mihi ancora	the Cross is my anchor
crux spes unica	the cross is the only hope (motto of Notre Dame University)
crux stellata	the cross with stars on its arms
cucullus non facit monachum	the cowl does not make the monk
cui bono?	whom will it benefit? who stands to gain?
cui Fortuna ipsa cedit	to whom fortune herself yields (Cicero)
cuilibet in arte sua perito credendum est	every skilled man is to be trusted in his own art
cui malo?	whom will it harm?
cui placet obliviscitur, cui dolet meminit	we forget our pleasures, we remember our sufferings (Cicero)
cuique suum	to each his own
cuius	of which
cuius regio eius religio	he who owns the region, his is the religion
cuius libet	of any that you please
cuius vis hominis est errare	it is natural for any man to make a mistake (Cicero)
culpa	fault
culpae poenae par esto	let the punishment fit the crime
culpa lata	gross negligence
culpa levis	ordinary negligence

culpam poena premit comes — punishment presses hard upon the heels of crime (Horace

cum — with

cum bona venia — with good favor

cum grano salis — with a grain of salt

cum laude — with praise; with distinction

cum multis aliis — with many others

cum notis variorum — with the notes of various critics

cum onere — with the burden (of proving a charge)

cum privilegio — with privilege; an authorized edition

cum tacent clamant — when they are silent, they cry out (Cicero)

cuneus cuneum trudit — a wedge drives a wedge

cupiditas ex homine, cupido ex stulto numquam tollitur — a man can be cured of his lust, but a fool can never be cured of his greed

cupido dominandi cunctis adfectibus flagrentior est — the lust for power inflames the heart more than any other passion (Tacitus)

curae leves loquuntur, ingentes stupent — slight griefs talk, great ones are speechless

cura facit canos — care brings gray hairs

cur ante tubam tremor occupat artus? — why should fear seize the limbs before the trumpet sounds? (Virgil)

curia — a court of law

curia advisari vult — the court wishes to be advised

curia Domini — the Lord's court

curia regis	the king's court
curiosa felicitas	painstaking spontaneity (Petronius)
currente calamo	with the pen running on; an afterthought
curriculum vitae	the courts of one's life; an academic resume
currus bovem trahit	the cart draws the ox
cursus curiae est lex curiae	the practice of the court is the law of the court
cursus honorum	course of honors leading to a high position
curta supellex	meager stock of furniture (knowledge)
custodia legis	in the custody of the law
custos	guardian
custos morum	a guardian of the manners
custos incorruptissimus	an incorruptible guardian
custos rotularum	guardian of the rolls; justice of the peace
cyathus	glassful
cyathus vinosus	glassful of wine

D

dabit deus his quoque finem
God will bring an end to this (Virgil)

dabit qui dedit
he who has given once will give (again)

da fidei quae fidei sunt
give to faith that which belongs to faith

da locum melioribus
give way to your betters (Terence)

damna minus consulta movent
losses to which we are accustomed affect us less deeply (Juvenal)

damnant quod non intelligunt
they condemn what they do not understand

damnosa hereditas
inheritance of damnation; ruinous legacy

damnum absque injuria
loss without injury, not subject to remedy

dante Deo
by the gift of God

dapes inemptae
unbought feasts; homegrown produce

dare pondus idonea fumo
fit only to give weight to smoke (Persius)

data et accepta
things given and received; expenses and income

data fata secutus
following what is decreed by fate (Virgil)

dat, donat, dicat	he gives, devotes, dedicates
date et dabitur vobis	give and it shall be given unto you (Vulgate)
date obolum Belisario	give a penny to Belisarius
dat veniam corvis, vexat censura columbas	the censures indulge the crows but harass the doves (Juvenal)
Davus sum, non Oedipus	I am Davus, not Oedipus (Terence)
de aequitate	in equity
de ambitu	in bribery
de asini umbra disceptare	to argue about the shadow of an ass (Disareli)
de auditu	from hearsay
De Beata Vita	On the Good Life (St. Augustine)
debellare superbos	to overthrow the proud (Virgil)
de bene esse	subject to conditions or provisions
debitum	debt
debitum naturae	debt of nature; death
de bona memoria	of good memory; of a sound mind
de bonis asportatis	of the goods carried away
de bonis non administratis	of the goods not yet administered
de bonis propriis	out of his own goods
de bono et malo	of good and bad; come what may
de bono gestu	for good behavior
decani	to be sung by the dean (antiphonal music)

decanus	dean; having supervision over ten people
decanta	pour off
deceptio visus	a deception of vision; optical illusion
decessit sine prole (D. S. P.)	died without children
decies repetita placebit	though ten times repeated, it will continue to please (Horace)
decipimur specie rectie	we are deceived by the semblance of what is right (Horace)
decipi quam fallere est tutius	it is safer to be deceived than to deceive
decipi frons prima multos	the first appearance deceives many
De Civitate Dei	On the City of God (St. Augustine)
de claro die	by the light of day
decori decus addit avito	he adds honor to the ancestral honor
decretum	a decree; a mandate
decubitus	lying down
decus et tutamen	honor and defense
de die in diem	from day to day; continuously
de duobus malis, minus est semper eligendum	of two evils, always choose the lesser one (Thomas à Kempis)
de facto	existing by fact
defectus sanguinis	failure to issue
deficit omne quod nascitur	everything that is born passes away (Quintilian)
de fide	of faith

de fide et officio judicis non recipitur quaestio — no question can be allowed concerning the faith and duty of the judge

definitum — a thing defined

de fumo in flammam — out of the smoke into the flame

degeneres animos timor arguit — fear betrays ignoble souls (Virgil)

de gratia — by favor

de gustibus non est disputandum — in matters of taste, there is no argument

Dei gratia — by the grace of God

Dei judicium — the judgment of God

de integro — from the beginning; one more time

dei penates — guardians of the household

Dei plena sunt omnia — all things are full of God

Dei Sponsa — The Bride of God (poem by Patmore)

Dei sub numine viget — it flourishes under the will of God (motto of Princeton University)

de jure — existing by lawful right

de lana caprina — about goat's wool; about worthless objects

delectando pariterque monendo — giving pleasure and at the same time instruction (Horace)

delenda est Carthago — Carthage must be destroyed (Cato the Elder)

deliciae humani generis — the delight of mankind (Emperor Titus)

delictum — offense

delineavit	he or she drew it
delirium tremens	alcoholic distress; delusions and trembling
delphinum natare doces	you are teaching a dolphin to swim
delphinum silvis appingit, fluctibus aprum	he portrays a dolphin in the woods and a wild boar on the waves (Horace)
de lunatico inquiriendo	a writ to inquire into the insanity of a person
dementia	insanity
dementia a potu	insanity from drinking
dementia praecox	insanity in adolescence
deme supercilio nubem	remove the cloud from your brow
de minimis	of the most insignificant things
de minimis non curat lex	the law does not concern itself with trifles
de mortuis nil nisi bonum	of the dead (say) nothing but good (Horace)
de nihilo nihil	nothing comes from nothing (Persius)
denique caelum	heaven at last (battle cry of the Crusaders)
denique non omnes eadem mirantur amantque	all men do not admire and love the same things (Horace)
de novo	new, fresh, renewed, to begin again
dente lupus, cornu taurus petit	the wolf attacks with his teeth, the bull with his horns (Horace
dente superbo	with a disdainful tooth (Horace)

dentur tales doses	give of such doses
Deo adjuvante non timendum	with God helping, nothing should be feared
Deo date	give unto God
deo dignus vindice nodus	a knot worthy of god to untie
Deo duce	with God as my leader
De duce, ferro comitante	with God as my leader and my sword as my companion
Deo et regi fidelis	faithful to God and king
Deo favente	with God's favor
Deo gratias (D.G.)	thanks be to God
Deo juvante	with God's help (motto of Monaco)
de omnibus rebus et quibusdam aliis	concerning all things and certain other matters; circumlocution
de omni re scibili et quibusdam aliis	concerning everything knowable and a few other things besides
Deo Optimo maximo (D. O. M.)	for God, the best and greatest (moto of the Benedictines)
Deo, patriae, amicis	for God, fatherland, and friends
deorum cibus est	it is food for the gods
deos enim reliquos accepimus, Caesares dedimus	the gods were handed down to us, but we created the Caesars ourselves
dei fortioribus adsunt	the gods aid the stronger (Tacitus)
Deo volente (D. V.)	God willing

de pilo pendet	it hangs by a hair; reaching a critical stage
de plano	with ease; without difficulty
de praesenti	for the present
deprendi miserum est	it is wretched to be detected
De Profundis	from the depths; out of despair (Psalm 130)
de proprio motu	of one's own motion; spontaneously
de rubus	of things
De Rerum Natura	On the Nature of Things (Lucretius)
desideratum	a thing much desired or needed
Desideria	Longings (poem by Wordsworth)
designatum	that which is designated
desinit in piscem mulier formosa superne	a woman, beautiful above, with a fish's tail (Horace)
desipere in loco	it is sweet to relax at the proper time (Horace)
desuetudo	disuse, no longer active
desunt cetera	the remainder is lacking
desunt multa	many things are lacking
de te fabula narratur	the story is told of you (Horace)
de tempore in tempus	from time to time
detur aliquando otium quiesque fessis	let ease and rest be sometimes granted to the weary (Seneca)
detur digniori	let it be given to the more worthy

detur pulchriori	let it be given to the fairer
Deum cole, regem serva	worship God and serve the king
Deus avertat	God forbid
Deus det	God grant
Deus est regit qui omnia	there is a God who rules all things
Deus est summum bonum	God is the chief good
deus ex machina	god from a machine; a person who intervenes to solve a problem at the last minute
Deus gubernat navem	God steers the ship
Deus lux Mea	God is my light (motto of the Catholic University of America)
Deus misereatur	may God have mercy (Psalm 67)
Deus nobiscum, quis contra?	God with us, who can be against us?
Deus nobis fiducia	God is our trust (motto of George Washington University)
Deus nobis haec otia fecit	God has brought for us this repose (Virgil)
Deus providebit	God will provide
Deus tecum	may God be with you (singular)
Deus vobiscum	may God be with you (plural)
Deus vult	God wills it (motto of the First Crusade)
de verbo in verbum	word for word
de verborum signifacatione	on the signifiance of words

dextras dare	to give right hands; to shake hands
dextro tempore	at the right time (Horace)
dicamus bona verba	let us speak words of good omen (Terence)
dic bona fide	tell me in good faith (Plautus)
dicere quae puduit, scribere iussit amor	what modesty forbade me to say, love has commanded me to write (Ovid)
dicitur	it is said; they say
dictis facta suppetant	let deeds correspond to words
dictum ac factum	(no sooner) said than done (Terence)
dictum de dicto	report upon hearsay
dictum de omni et nullo	maxim of all and nothing
dictum sapienti sat est	a word to the wise is sufficient
diebus alternis	every other day
diebus tertiis	every third day
diem ex die	day by day; continuously
diem perdidi	I have lost a day (Emperor Titus)
dies	day; daily
Dominica	Sunday
Lunae	Monday
Martis	Tuesday
Mercurii	Wednesday
Iovis	Thursday
Veneris	Friday
Saturni	Saturday
dies a quo	day from which

dies datus	a given day
dies dominicus	the Lord's day
dies faustus	a day bringing good fortune; auspicious day
dies infaustus	a day bringing bad fortune; an unlucky day
Dies Irae	Day of Wrath (hymn for the Requiem Mass)
dies juridicus	a day on which the court is in session
dies non	a day on which no business can be transacted
dies non juridicus	a day on which the court is not in session
difficiles nugae	laborious trifles (Martial)
difficilia quae pulchra	things that are excellent are difficult
digito monstrari	to be pointed out with fingers (Persius)
dignus vindice nodus	a knot worthy of such a liberator (Horace)
di (also dii)	gods (singular deus)
di immortales virtutem approbare, non adhibere debent	we may expect the gods to approve virtue, but not to endow us with it
di majores	the greater gods; men of eminence
di meliora	heaven send us better times
dimidium facti qui coepit habet	he who has begun has the work half done (Horace)
dimidius	one-half
di minores	the lesser gods; men of lesser merit

di penates	the household gods
di pia facta vident	the gods see virtuous deeds (Ovid)
dirige nos Domine	direct us, O Lord
dirigo	I direct (motto of Maine)
diruit, aedificat, mutat quadrata rotundis	he pulls down, he builds up, he changes square things to round (Horace)
dis aliter visum	the gods thought otherwise (Virgil)
disce pati	learn to endure
discere et docere	to learn and to teach
discere docendo	to learn through teaching
disciplina praesidium civitatis	instruction is the safeguard of the state (motto of the University of Texas)
dis ducibus	under the direction of the gods
disjecta membra	scattered limbs; fragments of a work
disjecta membra poetae	limbs of the dismembered poet (Horace)
dispendia morae	loss of time (Virgil)
disputandi pruritus ecclesiarum scabies	an itch for disputation is the incurable disease of the church
ditat Deus	God enriches (motto of Arizona)
dives agris, dives positis in faenore nummis	rich in lands, rich in money lent out at interest (Horace)
divide in partes aequales	divide into equal parts
divide et impera	divide in order to conquer

divide et regna	divide and rule (Machiavelli)
divina natura dedit agros, ars humana aedificavit urbes	divine nature gave us the fields, human skill built the cities (Terentius)
divinae particula aurae	particle of divine spirit (Horace)
divitiae virum faciunt	riches make the man
dixi	I have spoken; I will say no more
docendo discitur	one learns by teaching
docendo discimus	we learn by teaching
doce ut discas	teach in order to learn
doctor utriusque legis	doctor of both laws (canon and civil)
doctus cum libro	learned with a book; having book learning
doctus cum multis libris	learned with many books; a polymath
dolium volvitur	an empty cask is easily rolled
dolus	deceit; fraud
dolus bonus	permissible deceit
dolus malus	unlawful deceit
Domine, dirige nos	Lord, direct us (motto of London)
Dominica palmarum	Palm Sunday
dominium eminens	eminent domain
Domino optimo maximo (D.O.M.)	to the Lord, best and greatest
Dominus	the Lord
Dominus illuminatio mea	the Lord is my light (motto of Oxford)
Dominus providebit	the Lord will provide
Dominus vobiscum	may the Lord be with you

domus et placens uxor	a home and a pleasing wife (Horace)
Domus Procerum	the House of Lords
donec eris felix, multos numerabis amicos	as long as you are fortunate, you will have many friends (Ovid)
dono dedit	he or she gave as a gift
dormitat Homerus	(even) Homer sleeps
do ut des	I give so that you may give
do ut facias	I give so that you may do
dramatis personae	list of characters in a play
duabus sellis sedere	to sit in two saddles; to wear two hats
duas tantum res anxius optat, panem et circenses	two things only do the people earnestly desire, bread and the circus (Juvenal)
duces tecum	you shall bring it with you; subpoena
ducit amor patriae	the love of country leads (me)
ductus	style; manner
ductus figuratus	figurative or indirect style
ductus simplex	straightforward or simple style
ductus subtilis	subtle or deceiving style
ducunt volentem fata, nolentem trahunt	fate leads the willing soul, but drags along the unwilling one (Seneca)
dulce bellum inexpertis	war is sweet to those who have never fought
dulce est desipere in loco	it is sweet to relax at the proper time

dulce et decorum est pro patria mori	it is sweet and proper to die for one's country
dulce quod utile	what is useful is sweet
dulces moriens reminiscitur Argos	as he dies, he remembers his beloved Argos (Virgil)
dulce sodalicium	sweet companionship; pleasant association
dulcis amor patriae	sweet is the love of one's country
dulcis domus	sweet home
dum	while; on the condition that
dum docent, discunt	while they teach, they learn (Seneca)
dum fortuna fuit	while fortune lasted
dum inter homines sumus, colamus humanitatem	so long as we live among men, let us cherish humanity (Seneca)
dum loquimor fugerit invida aetas	even as we speak, time speeds swiftly away (Horace)
dum loquor, hora fugit	time is flying while I speak (Ovid)
dum solus	while single
dum spiro, spero	while I breathe, I hope (a motto of South Carolina)
dum tacent clamant	though they are silent, they cry aloud
dum vita est spes est	while there's life, there's hope
dum vitant stulti vitia in contraria currunt	in shunning vices, fools run to the opposite extreme (Horace)
dum vivimus, vivamus	while we live, let us live (Catullus)

duplici spe uti	to have a double hope
dura lex sed lex	the law is hard, but it is the law
durante	during
durante absentia	during absence
durante bene placito	during good pleasure; as long as one wishes
durante dolore	while pain lasts
durante minore aetate	during minority, at an early age
durante vita	during one's life
durate et vosmet rebus servate secundis	carry on and preserve yourselves for better times (Virgil)
durum hoc est sed ita lex scripta est	this is harsh but the law is written
dux femina facti	a woman was the leader in the deed (Virgil)
dux gregis	leader of the flock

E

ecce	behold
ecce agnus Dei	behold the Lamb of God
ecce homo	behold the man (Christ in crown of thorns)
ecce quam bonum	behold how good (Psalm 133)
ecce quomodo moritur	behold the way of death
ecce signum	behold the sign; here is the proof
e contra	on the other hand
e contrario	on the contrary
editio cum notis variorum	an edition with notes of various writers
editio cum privilegio	a licensed and authorized edition of a book
editio princeps	first printed edition of a text
editio vulgata	the common edition for the majority
effectus sequitur causam	the effect follows the cause
effugere non potes necessitates, potes vincere	you cannot escape necessities, but you can overcome them (Seneca)
e flamma petere cibum	to snatch food out of the flame (Terence)
ego et rex meus	my king and I (Cardinal Wolsey)

egomet mihi ignosco — I myself pardon myself (Horace)

ego spem pretio non emo — I do not purchase hope for a price (Terence)

eheu, fugaces labuntur anni — alas, the fleeting years go by (Horace)

ei incumbit probatio qui dicit non qui negat — the proof lies upon the one who affirms, not the one who denies

ejectamenta — ejected matter, worthless items

ejusdem farinae — of the same flour; persons of the same nature

ejusdem generis — of the same kind; of the same class

elapso tempore — the time having elapsed

elephantem ex musca facis — you are making an elephant out of a fly

elixir vitae — elixir of life

emeritus — one having served his time

emollit mores nec sinit esse feros — it makes gentle the character and does not allow it to be unrefined (Ovid)

empta dolore experientia docet — experience teaches when bought with pain

emptor — buyer, purchaser

emulsio — an emulsion

e necessitate — from necessity; having no alternative

enim vero di nos quasi pilas homines habent — the gods use mortals as their playthings

ens a se — a being in itself

Ens Entium — the Supreme Being

ense et aratro	with sword and plow
ense petit placidam sub libertate quietem	by the sword she seeks peaceful repose under liberty (motto of Massachusetts)
ens legis	a creature of the law
ens rationis	a rational being
ens realissimum	the most real being
entia non sunt multiplicanda praeter necessitatem	things are not to be multiplied unless necessary (Occam's Razor)
eo animo	with that intention
eo instante	at that moment
eo ipso	by that itself; by that fact
eo loco	at that very place
eo nomine	under the name
Epicuri de grege porcus	a hog from the grove of Epicurus; an exquisite meal (Horace)
e pluribus unum	one out of many (motto of the United States)
epulis accumbere divis	to recline at the feasts of the gods (Virgil)
e re nata	under the present circumstance
ergo	therefore
eripuit caelo fulmen sceptrumque tyrannis	he snatched the thunderbolt from heaven and the sceptor from tyrants (Benjamin Franklin)
errare est humanum	to err is human (Alexander Pope)
erratum	an error in printing or writing (pl. errata)

erubuit, salva res est	he blushed, the affair is safe (Terence)
eruditio et religio	learning and religion (motto of Duke University)
esse	to be; being; existence
esse est percipi	to be is to be perceived (Bishop Berkeley)
esse quam videri	to be rather than to seem (motto of North Carolina)
esse quam videri bonus malebat	he preferred to be good rather than to merely seem good (Sallust)
esse quid	to be; being thus so
est ars etiam male dicendi	there is an art even to malediction
est autem vis legem simulans	violence may also simulate the law
est brevitate opus, ut currat sententia	terseness is needed so that the thought may run free (Horace)
est deus in nobis	there is a god within us (Ovid)
est et fideli tuta silentio merces	loyalty has its reward secure (Horace)
est modus in rebus	there is a proper measure in things (Horace)
esto perpetua	may she live forever (motto of Idaho)
esto perpetuum	let it be everlasting
esto quod esse videris	be what you seem to be
est quaedam flere voluptas	there is a certain pleasure in crying (Ovid)
est unusquisque faber ipsae suae fortunae	every man is the creator of his own fortune

et alia; et alii (et al.)	and other things; and other people
et alibi	and elsewhere
et campose ubi Troia fruit	and the plains where Troy once was (Virgil)
et cetera (etc.)	and the rest; and so forth
et cum spiritu tuo	and with your spirit
et decus et pretium recti	both the ornament and reward of virtue
et discere et rerum exquire re causas	both to learn and to investigate the causes of things (motto of Georgia)
et ego in Arcadia	and I too (Death) have been in Arcadia
E Tenebris	Out of the Darkness (poem by Oscar Wilde)
et genus et formam regina pecunia donat	money, like the queen, gives them both rank and beauty (Horace)
et genus et virtus, nisi cum re, vilior alga est	without substance, honor and valor are more worthless than seaweed (Horace)
et hoc genus omne	and everything of the kind
etiam atque etiam	again and again
etiam peribant ruinae	even the ruins have perished (Lucan)
etiam sapientibus cupido gloriae novissima exuitur	the desire for glory is the last infirmity to be cast off even by the wise (Tacitus)
et id genus omne	and everything of the kind

et mihi res, non me rebus subjungere conor	I suit life to myself, not myself to life (Horace)
et nos quoque tela sparsimus	we too have hurled weapons
et nunc et semper	now and always
et passim	and everywhere; scattered thought
et sceleratis sol oritur	the sun shines even on the wicked (Seneca)
et sequens (et seq.)	and the following
et sic de ceteris	and so the rest
et sic de similibus	and so of similar things (or people)
et sic fecit	and he or she did so
et tollens vacuum plus nimio Gloria verticem	Vainglory, who lifts her proud head too high
et tu Brute	and you too, Brutus (Julius Caesar)
et uxor (et ux.)	and wife
eventus stultorum magister	the result is the instructor of fools (Livy)
ex abrupto	without preparation
ex abundante cautela	from excessive caution
ex abundantia	out of the abundance
ex abusu non arguitur in usum	from the abuse of a thing there is no arguing against its use
ex acervo	out of a heap
ex adverso	from the opposite side
ex aequo et bono	according to justice and right
ex animo	from the heart; sincerely
ex auctoritate commissa	by virtue of my authority
ex bona fide	out of one's honor; from good faith

ex capite	out of the head; from memory
ex cathedra	from the seat; a position of authority
excelsior	ever higher (motto of the State of New York)
exceptio probat regulam de rebus non exceptis	the exception proves the rule as to things not excepted
exceptis exicipiendibus	things excluded which should be excluded
excerpta	selections or excerpts
excitari, non hebescere	to be excited, not dull
ex commodo	from convenience
ex concesso	from what has been conceded
ex contractu	matter arising out of a contract
excudit	he or she cast it
ex curia	from the court
ex delicto	matter arising out of the crime
ex dono	by gift of; donated by
ex dono Dei	by the gift of God
exeat	he or she may go out; allowing student to be absent
exegi monumentum aere perennius	I have raised a monument more durable than bronze (Horace)
exempla sunt odiosa	examples are odious
exempli gratia (e.g.)	for the sake of example
exemplum	sample; copy; model
exequatur	it may be executed

exeunt	they go out; the players leave the stage
exeunt omnes	all the players leave the stage
exercitatio optimus es magister	practice is the best teacher
ex facie	from the face of
ex facto	from the fact or act
ex facto jus oritur	the law arises out of the fact
ex fide fortis	strength through faith
ex granis fit acervus	many grains make a heap
ex gratia	as an act of grace; out of one's favor
exhibeatur	let it be given
exit	he or she goes out; player leaves the stage
exitus acta probat	the end justifies the means (Ovid)
ex lege	arising from the law
ex libris	from the library of (used on bookplates)
ex longinquo	from a distance
ex malis moribus bonae leges natae sunt	from bad usages, good laws have been born
ex mera gratia	through mere favor
ex mero motu	our of simple impulse; spontaneously
ex modo praescripto	as directed
ex more	according to custom
ex natura rei	from the nature of things
ex necessitate rei	from the necessity of the case
ex nihilo	from nothing

ex nihilo nihil fit	from nothing, nothing can be made (Lucretius)
ex officio	by virtue of one's office
Ex Ore Infantium	Out of the Mouth of Babes (Francis Thompson)
ex ore parvulorum veritas	out of the mouth of little children (comes) truth
exorire alquis nortis ex ossibus ultor	rise up from my dead bones, avenger (Virgil)
ex parte	from one side only; partisan
ex pede Herculem	to measure Hercules from his foot; from the sample we are able to estimate the whole
expende Hannibalem	weigh (the dust of) Hannibal (Juvenal)
experientia docet	experience teaches
experientia docet stultos	experience teaches fools
experimentum crucis	a crucial experiment
experto credito	trust in one who has experience
expertus metuit	having had experience, he is afraid (Horace)
explicit	it ends here
explorant adversa viros	misfortune tries men
ex post facto	after the fact; in retrospect
expressio unius est exclusio alterius	the expression of one thing excludes others
expressis verbis	in express terms
ex professo	in an open manner
ex proposito	of a set purpose; by design
ex propriis	from one's own resources

ex proprio motu	of one's own accord; voluntarily
ex quocunque capite	for whatever reason
ex relatione	upon relation or report
ex tacito	in a tacit manner
ex tempore	spontaneously, without preparation
ex silentio	in consequence of no contrary evidence
exinctus amabitur idem	the same one will be loved after he's dead
extortor bonorum legumque contortor	one who extorts good citizens and twists the laws (Terence)
extra modum	beyond measure
extra muros	beyond the walls
extra pecuniam non est vita	without money there is no life
ex turpi causa non oritur actio	no immoral matter can lead to a legal action
ex ungue leonem	from the claw (we may judge) a lion; from a sample we may judge the whole
ex uno disce omnes	from one, learn of all; deductive reasoning
eiurare patriam	to renounce one's country
ex usu	of use; advantageous
ex vi termini	from the force of the term
ex voluntate	as a volunteer, without obligation
ex voto	out of a vow; in pursuance of a vow

F

fabas indulcet fames	hunger sweetens beans
faber est quisque fortunae suae	every man is architect of his own fortune
fabula	a comedy or farce
fabula Atellana	Atellan farce
fabula crepidata	Roman tragedy based upon Greek models
fabulae amatoriae	love stories, often with tragic plots
fabulae palliatae	cloak comedy, as of Plautus and Terence
facere sacramentum	to take an oath
facere totum	to do everything
facies non omnibus una nec diversa tamen	the features are not the same in all respects, nor are they different (Ovid)
facile est inventis addere	it is easy to add to things already invented
facile largire de alieno	it is easy to be generous with things of another person
facile omnes quom valemus recta consilia aegrotis damus	when we are healthy, we all have advice for those who are sick
facile princeps	easily first; number one in the field
facilis descensus Averno	the descent to hell is easy (Virgil)

facilius est multa facere quam diu	it is easier to do many things than to do one thing for a long time
facinus quos inquinant aequat	guilt equates all who share in guilt
facio ut des	I do so that you may give
facio ut facias	I do so that you may do
facit indignatio versum	indignation produces verse (Juvenal)
facta armorum	facts of arms
fact non verba	deeds not words; action not speeches
facta sunt potentiora verbis	facts are more powerful than words
factotum	one who does everything; handyman
factum est	it is done, it is complete
factum infectum fieri nequit	a thing done cannot be undone
factum probandum	the fact of a case to be proved
factum probans	facts tending to prove other facts
fac ut sciam	make me know; make me aware
faenum habet in cornu, longe fuge	he has hay on his horn, keep your distance (reference to a charging bull) (Horace)
faex populi	the dregs of the people; the rabble (Cicero)
fallacia consequentis	fallacy of the consequence
fallentis semitia vitae	the narrow path of a private life (Horace)
falsa demonstratio	false designation; erroneous description

falsa lectio	false reading; erroneous interpretation
falsi crimem	the crime of falsification
falsus in uno, falsus in omnibus	false in one thing, false in everything
fama clamosa	noisy rumor; public scandal
fama mala quo non aliud velocius ullum	there is nothing swifter than an evil rumor (Virgil)
famam extendere factis	to make known his fame by deeds (Virgil)
fama nihil est celerius	nothing is swifter than a rumor
fama semper vivat	may his or her good name live forever
fama volat	rumor travels fast (adapted from Virgil)
fames optimum condimentum	hunger is the best seasoning
familiares regis	persons of the king's household
famosus libellus	a slanderous or libelous letter
farrago libelli	miscellaneous contents of a book
fari quae sentiat	to say what one feels (Horace)
fas est et ab hoste doceri	it is right to learn even from an enemy
fasti	calendar of events
fasti et nefasti dies	lucky and unlucky days
Fata obstant	the Fates willed otherwise
Fata viam invenient	the Fates will find a way

Fata volentem docunt, nolentem trahunt	the Fates lead the willing and drag those who are unwilling
fatua mulier	a foolish woman; a prostitute
favete linguis	favor with your tongue; say nothing bad lest you displease the gods (Horace)
fax mentis incendium gloriae	the passion for glory is fire for the mind
fecit	he or she made it
felicitas habet multos amicos	prosperity has many friends
feliciter	happily; fortunately
felix culpa	fortunate fault
felix qui nihil debet	happy is he who owes nothing
felix qui potuit rerum cognoscere causas	fortunate is he who understands the causes of things (Virgil)
felo de se	one who kills himself doing an illegal act
ferae naturae	wild beasts; undomesticated animals
fere libenter homines id quod volunt credunt	men readily believe what they want to believe (Julius Caesar)
ferrea non venerem sed praedam saecula laudant	the iron age celebrates not love but the acquisition of material possessions
fervens	boiling
fervens difficili bile tumet iecur	my liver (seat of passion) swells with burning wrath (Horace)

fervet opus	the work boils (Virgil)
fessus viator	weary traveler
festina lente	make haste slowly (Emperor Augustus)
fiat	let it be made
fiat Dei voluntas	may God's will be done
fiat experimentum in corpore	let one experiment on a body
fiat haustus	let a draught be made
fiat justitia	let justice be done
fiat justitia, ruat caelum	let justice be done, even though the heavens fall
fiat lux	let there be light (Genesis)
fiat mixtura	let a mixture be made
fiat potio	let a portion be made
fiat voluntas tua	Thy will be done (Gospel of Matthew)
ficta voluptatis causa sint proxima veris	fictions should approximate the truth in order to please
fictilia	pottery
fictilis	made of pottery
fictio cedit veritati	fiction yields to the truth
fide et amore	by faith and love
fide et fortitudine	by fidelity and fortitude
fidei est coticula crux	the Cross is the touchstone of faith
Fidei Defensor (F.D.)	defender of faith (motto of the sovereigns of England since Henry VIII)
fideli certa merces	to the faithful, reward is certain
fidelis ad urnam	faithful to the urn; faithful until death

fideliter	faithfully
fide, non armis	by faith, not by arms
fides ante intellectum	faith before understanding
fides, sed cui vide	trust, but watch out to whom
fides et justitia	faith and justice
fides et veritas	faith and truth
fides facit fidem	faith creates faith
fides non timet	faith does not fear
fides probata coronat	approved faith confers a crown
fides Punica	Punic faith; treacherous faith
fides servanda est	faith must be kept
fidus Achates	faithful companion (Virgil)
fidus et audax	faithful and courageous
fieri facias	writ authorizing execution of a judgment
figura causae	stylistic pattern of a speech
filius	a son
filius est pars patris	a son is part of the father
filius nullius	son of nobody; bastard
filius populi	son of the people
filius terrae	son of the earth; a serf
finem respice	look to the end; consider the end
finis coronat opus	the end crowns the work
fit via vi	a way is made by force
flagrante bello	in the midst of the war
flagrante delicto	in the heat of the crime

flamma fumo est proxima	fire is very close to smoke
flebile ludibrium	a tragic farce
flectere si nequeo superos, Acheronta movebo	if I can't bend heaven, then I will move hell (Virgil)
flecti, non frangi	to be bent, not broken
floreat	may it flourish
floreat Etona	may Eton flourish (motto of Eton)
flores	flowers
flores curat Deus	God cares for flowers
florilegium	a bunch of flowers; anthology or collection
floruit (fl.)	he or she flourished (during this period)
flosculi sententiarum	flowers of thought
fluctuat nec mergitur	it is tossed by the waves, but does not sink (motto of Paris)
folio recto	on the front of the page
folio verso	on the back of the page
fons et origo	the source and origin
fons malorum	the fountain of evils
fons vitae	fountain of life
forensis strepitus	the clamor of the forum
forma bonum fragile est	beauty is a fragile good (Ovid)
forma flos, fama flatus	beauty is a flower, fame is a breath
forsan et haec olim meminisse juvabit	perhaps this will be a pleasure to look back on one day (Virgil)
fortem posce animum	pray for a strong spirit (Juvenal)

forte scutum, salus ducum	a strong shield is the safety of our leaders
fortes fortuna iuvat	fortune favors the brave (Terence)
forti et fideli nihil difficile	to the brave and faithful, nothing is difficult
fortis cadere, cedere non potest	brave men may fall, but cannot yield
fortis et fidelis	brave and faithful
fortiter et recte	bravely and rightly
fortiter, fideliter, feliciter	bravely, faithfully, happily
fortiter geret crucem	he will bravely bear the cross
fortiter in re, suaviter in modo	resolutely in action, gently in manner
fortudine et prudetia	by courage and prudence
fortitudini	for bravery
fortuna caeca est	fortune is blind
fortunae cetera mando	I commit the rest to fortune
forunae filius	a son of fortune (Horace)
fortuna favet fatuis	fortune favors fools
fortuna favet fortibus	fortune favors the strong
fortuna fortes iuvat	fortune helps the brave
fortuna fortes metuir, ignavos premit	fortune fears the brave, overwhelms the cowardly (Seneca)
fortunam citius reperias quam retineas	it is easier to meet with good fortune than to hold on to it
fortuna mea in bello campo	my fortune in a fair field
fortuna meliores sequitur	fortune follows the better man (Sallust)

fortuna multis dat nimiun, nulli satis — to many fortune gives too much, to none does he give enough (Martial)

fortuna nimium quem favet stultum facit — fortune makes a fool of one whom she favors too much (Publius Syrus)

fortuna sequatur — let fortune follow

fortuna vitrea est: tum cum splendet frangitur — fortune is like glass: it is most easily shattered when it is the brightest

forum non conveniens — an inconvenient court or place

fossoribus orti — risen from ditch diggers; of humble origin

frangas, non flectes — you may break me, but you will not bend me

fraus est celare fraudem — it is fraud to conceal a fraud

fraus pia — a pious fraud

fraus Punica — Punic fraud; treacherous deceit

frons est animi ianua — the forehead is the door of the mind (Cicero)

fronti nulla fides — do not trust in appearance (Juvenal)

fructus industriales — produce of the land resulting from manual labor

fructus naturales — produce of the land which grows naturally

fructu non foliis arborem aestima — judge a tree by its fruit, not by its leaves (Phaedrus)

fruges consumere nati — born to consume the fruits of the earth

fruimur pro iucunditate	let us enjoy things for pleasure
frustra laborat qui omnibus placere studet	he labors in vain who tries to please everyone
fugaces labuntur anni	the fleeting years go by
fugit hora	the hour flies
fugit irreparabile tempus	time is irretrievably flying (Virgil)
fuit Ilium	Troy has been; Troy is no more (Virgil)
fumus et opes strepitusque Romae	the smoke, the wealth and the clamor of Rome (Juvenal)
functus officio	having performed the duties of his office
fundamentum divisionis	principles according to which a genus is divided into a species
fundamentum iustitiae est fides	the foundation of justice is good faith (Cicero)
furor arma ministrat	rage supplies arms (Virgil)
furor loquendi	a rage for speaking
furor poeticus	a poetic frenzy
furor scribendi	a rage for writing

G

gaudemus igitur	therefore let us rejoice
gaudet tentamine virtus	virtue rejoices in trial
gaudium certaminis	the joy of the struggle
generales	general principles
genius loci	spirit of a place; prevailing atmosphere
gens togata	nation of togas; Roman citizens; civilians
genus	class of things sharing certain attributes
genus est mortis male vivere	to live an evil life is a type of death (Ovid)
genus irritabile vatum	the irritable race of poets (Horace)
Gesta Romanorum	Deeds of the Romans
glebae ascriptus	attached to the soil
Gloria	Glory
Gloria in Excelsis Deo	Glory to God on high (the greater doxology)
Gloria Patri	Glory to the Father (the lesser doxology)
Gloria Tibi, Domine	Glory be to Thee, O Lord
gloria virtutis umbra	glory is the shadow of virtue
gradatim	by steps; by degrees
gradatim vincimus	we conquer by degrees
gradus ad Parnassum	a step toward Parnassus
Graeculus esuriens	a hungry Greek (Juvenal)

grammatici certant adhuc sub iudice lis est	scholars dispute and the case is still before the court (Horace)
gratia Dei	by the Grace of God
gratia et veritas	grace and truth
gratia gratiam parit	kindness produces kindness
gratia placendi	the grace of pleasing
gratias agere	to give thanks
gratias tibi ago	I give thanks to you
gratior et pulchro veniens in corpore virtus	virtue and worth win more favor than beautiful form (Virgil)
gratis	free, at no cost
gratis dictum	an unsubstantiated assertion
graviora manent	worse things remain (Virgil)
graviora quaedam sunt remedia periculis	some remedies are worse than the disease (Publius Syrus)
gravis ira regum est semper	the wrath of kings is always severe (Seneca)
gravissimum est imperium consuetudinis	the power of custom is the strongest
gregatim	in flocks or herds
grex venalis	a venal gathering

H

habeas corpus — you have the body; a legal writ

habeas corpus ad subjiciendum — writ requiring presentation of the person

habemus confitentem reum — we have an accused person who pleads guilty (Cicero)

habendum et tenendum — having and holding

habentes homines — men of substance

habent sua fata libelli — books have their own destiny (Terentius)

habere et dispertire — to have and to distribute

habere, non haberi — to hold, not to be held

habet — he or she has it

habet et musca splenem — even a fly has anger

hac lege — under this law: under this condition

hac mercede placet — these terms are pleasing to me

hac urgeit lupus hac canis — on one side a wolf threatens, on the other side a dog threatens (Horace)

haec est conventio — this is an agreement

haec generi incrementa fides — this faith will augment our people

haec olim meminisse iuvabit — (even) these things will be a pleasure to remember one day (Virgil)

haec tibi dona fero — I bear these gifts to you (motto of Newfoundland)

hae nugae in seria ducent mala — these trifles will lead to serious evils (Horace)

haerent infixi pectore vultus — his looks are imprinted on her breast (Virgil)

Hannibal ad portas — Hannibal is at the gates (Cicero)

haud ignota loquor — I speak of things by no means unknown

haud longis intervallis — at intervals by no means long

haud passibus aequis — with unequal steps (Virgil)

helluo librorum — a devourer of books; a bookworm

heredis fletus sub persona risus est — the tears of an heir are mere laughter under a veil

hereditas damnosa — a burdensome inheritance

heres — an heir

heres est alter ipse — an heir is another self

heroum filii — sons of heroes (motto of Wellington College)

hesterni quirites — citizens of yesterday; freed slaves (Persius)

heu nihil invitis fas quemquam fidere divis — one cannot trust the gods for anything once they are against you (Virgil)

heu pietas heu prisca fides — alas for pity, alas for ancient faith (Virgil)

hiatus valde deflendus	a much regretted gap or deficiency
hic domus, haec patria est	here is our home, this is our country (Virgil)
hic et nunc	here and now
hic et ubique	here and everywhere
hic et ubique terrarum	here and everywhere throughout the world (motto of the Univeristy of Paris)
hic finis fandi	here the speech ended (Virgil)
hic funis nihil attraxit	this line has not attracted any fish
hic jacet	here lies (on tombstones)
hic jacet sepultus	here lies buried
hic jacet lepus	here lies the hare (the difficulty)
hic sepultus	here is buried
hinc illae lacrimae	hence these tears; cause of the disaster
hinc lucem et pocula sacra	from hence (we receive) light and sacred libations (motto of Cambridge)
his non obstantibus	notwithstanding these things
hi sunt inimici pessimi fronte hilaro	one's worst enemies are those whose faces are cheerful
hi testes	these are witnesses
hoc age	do this; apply yourself to this
hoc anno	in this year
hoc est	this is

hoc erat in more majorum	this was in the manner of our ancestors
hoc erat in votis	this was what I wished (Horace)
hoc est vivere bis vita posse priore frui	to live twice is to make useful profit of one's past (Martial)
hoc genus omne	all the people of that type (Horace)
hoc habet	he has it; he is a hit
hoc illis narro qui me non intelligunt	I am telling my tale to people who do not understand me (Virgil)
hoc indictum volo	I wish this statement to be withdrawn
hoc loco	in this place
hoc mense	in this month
hoc monumentum posuit	he or she erected this monument
hoc nocte	this night; tonight
hoc nomine	in this name
hoc opus, hic labor est	this is work, this is labor
hoc opus, hoc studium	this work, this pursuit
hoc quaere	look for this
hoc sensu	in this sense
hoc sustinete, maius ne veniat malum	endure this evil, lest a greater one should come to you (Phaedrus)
hoc tempore	at this time
hoc tempore obsequium amicos, veritas odium parit	today flattery wins friends, truth begets hatred (Terence)
hoc titulo	under this title
hoc verbo	under this word
hoc volo	this I wish

hoc volo, sic iubeo, sit pro ratione voluntas	this I wish, thus I command, let my will stand for my reason (Juvenal)
hodie mihi, cras tibi	today to me, tomorrow to you
hodie, non cras	today, not tomorrow
homagium reddere	to render homage
hominum causa jus constitutum	law is established for the benefit of man
hominem quaero	I am looking for a man (Phaedrus on Diogenes)
homini amico et familiari non est mentiri meum	I do not lie to my friends or family (Lucilius)
homo additus naturae	man added to nature (Francis Bacon)
homo antiqua virtute ac fide	a man of ancient virtue and loyalty
homo doctus in se semper divitas habet	a learned man always has wealth within himself
homo erectus	early species of man able to stand on two feet
homo faber	man the maker
homo homini aut deus aut lupus	man is either a wolf or a god to other men (Erasmus)
homo homini deus est si suum officium sciat	man is a god to man when he recognizes his duty to others
homo homini lupus	man is a wolf to his fellow man (Plautus)
homo multarum litterarum	a man of many letters

homo nullis coloris	man of no color; one who does not commit
homo rationalis	rational man; man as a cognitive being
homo sapiens	wise man: man as a member of human species
homo sum; humani nil a me alienum puto	I am a man; I regard nothing that concerns man as foreign to my interests (Terence)
homo totiens moritur quotiens amittit suos	a man dies as many times as he loses a dear friend
homo trium litterarum	a man of three letters; a thief
homo unius libri	man of one book; one educated by narrow means
homo vitae commodatus non donatus	a man is lent to life, not given (Publius Syrus)
homunculi quanti sunt	what unimportant creatures men are (Plautus)
homunculus	imaginary tiny man residing within a person
honesta mors turpi vita potior	an honorable death is better than a vile life (Tacitus)
honesta quam splendida	honorable things rather than brilliant things
honeste vivere	to live honestly
honorarium donum	an honorary gift; gratuitous payment
honores mutant mores	honors change manners
honor est a Nilo	honor is from the Nile

honoris causa	for the sake of honor; degree of recognition
honor virtutis praemium	honor is the reward of virtue (Cicero)
honos alit artes	honor nourishes the arts (Cicero)
honos habet onus	honor has its burden
hora decubitus	at the hour of bedtime
horae canonicae	canonical hours; hours of prayer
horae subsicivae	hours of leisure
horae unius spatio	in one hour's time
hora fugit	time flies; the hour passes quickly
horas non numero nisi serenas	I don't count the hours unless they're bright
hora somni	at the hour of sleep
horresco referens	I am horrified to relate (Virgil)
horribile dictu	horrible to relate
horribile visu	horrible to see
horror ubique	terror everywhere
hortus conclusus	enclosed garden; private sanctuary
hortus siccus	collection of dry plants; herbarium
hos ego versiculos feci, tulit alter honores	I wrote these lines, another has carried away the honors (Virgil)
hospes, hostis	stranger, enemy
hostis honori invidia	envy is the foe of honor
hostis humani generis	enemy of the human race
huius anni	of this year
huius mensis	of this month

humani generis	of the human race (Pope Pius XII)
humani nihil a me alienum puto	I consider nothing that relates to man foreign to me (Terrence)
humanius est deridere vitam quam deplorare	it is more appropriate for a man to laugh at life than to lament it (Seneca)
humanum amare est: humanum autem ignoscere est	to love is human; to indulge is human also
humanum est errare	to err is human
humiles laborant ubi potentes dissident	poor people suffer when the powerful disagree
hunc laborem sumas laudem qui tibi ac fructum ferat	accept work which brings praise and profit (Lucilius)
hunc tu caveto	beware of him
hunc tu, Romane, caveto	of him, Roman, beware (Horace)

I

iacta alea est

the die is cast (Julius Caesar, on crossing the Rubicon,49 B.C.)

iam proximus ardet Ucalegon

Ucalegon's house next door is burning (Virgil)

iam redit et virgo, redeunt Saturnia regna

now returns the Virgin, now the Golden age returns (Virgil)

iam satis

already enough

ianuae mentis

the doors of the mind

ianuis clausis

with closed doors

ibidem (ibid.)

the same text

idem

the same

idem quod

the same as

idem sonans

sounding the same as

idem velle atque idem nolle

to like and dislike the same things (Sallust)

ides

the fifteenth (or thirteenth) day of the month on the ancient Roman calendar

id est (i.e.)

that is

id genus omne

all that sort; everyone of that class

idoneus homo

the fit man; man of proven ability

ieiunus raro stomachus vulgaria temnit

the empty stomach seldom turns away food (Horace)

Iesus Hominum Salvator (I.H.S)	Jesus, Savior of mankind
Iesus Nazarenus Rex Iudaeorum	Jesus of Nazareth, King of the Jews
ignavis semper feriae sunt	to the lazy it is always a holiday
ignis aururn probat, miseria fortes viros	fire tests gold; adversity tests strong men (Seneca)
ignis fatuus	foolish fire; will-of-the-wisp
ignis iudicium	trial by fire
ignobilis vulgus	the ignoble crowd
ignorantia facti excusat, ignorantia iuris non excusat	ignorance of fact excuses one, ignorance of law does not excuse one
ignorantia legis non excusat	ignorance of the law is no excuse
ignorantia legis non exculpat	ignorance of the law does not free one from blame
ignorantia elenchi	an irrelevant argument or conclusion; a logical fallacy disproving a proposition
ignoscito saepe alteri nunquam tibi	forgive others often, forgive yourself never
ignoti nulla cupido	no desire exists for an unknown thing (Ovid)
ignotum per ignotius	explaining the unknown by means of something even more unknown
ignotus	unknown
Ilias malorum	an lliad of woes; multitude of misfortune

illaeso lumine solum	with undazzled eye to the sun
illotis manibus	with unwashed hands
imagines majorum	portraits of ancestors
imago pietatis	image of Christ standing upright in His tomb
imitatores, servum pecus	imitators, you servile herd (Horace)
immedicabile vulnus	an incurable wound (Ovid)
imo pectore	from the bottom of the heart
impari Marte	in unequal combat
impavidum ferient ruinae	the ruins of the world will not dismay him (Horace)
imperat aut servit collecta pecunia cuique	money saved either rules us or serves us (Horace)
imperator Dei gratia	emperor by the grace of God
imperiosus	imperious; haughty
imperium et libertas	empire and liberty
imperium in imperio	authority within another's jurisdiction
implicite	by implication
imponere Pelio Olympo	to pile Pelion on Olympus; to make matters much worse
impos animi	having no control over one's mind
impossibilium nulla obligatio est	no obligation to do the impossible is binding
impotens sui	having no control over one's self
imprimatur	official sanction for publication of text

imprimis	in first place
in absentia	in the absence of a particular person
in abstracto	in the abstract
in actu	in the act; in reality
in aeternum	in eternity; forever
in alio loco	in another place
in ambiguo	in doubt
in aqua scribis	you are writing in water
in arduis virtus	to have virtue in difficulties
in arena aedificas	you are building upon the sand
in armis	in arms
in articulo mortis	in the grasp of death; at the point of death
in banco	in full court
in banco regis	in the King's Bench
in beato omnia beata	with the blessed all things are blessed (Horace)
in bello parvis momentis magni casus intercedunt	in war great events are caused by small things (Julius Caesar)
in bonis	in the goods or property
in caelo quies	in heaven is rest
in caelo salus	in heaven is salvation
in camera	in a room; a meeting conducted in secret
in capite	in chief, reference to holder of estate
in cauda venenum	in the tail is the poison; beware of danger
Incarnatus	incarnate (section of the Nicene Creed)

incessu patuit dea	by her walk the goddess was revealed (Virgil)
in Christi nomine	in the name of Christ
incidis in Scyllam cupiens vitare Charybdim	you fall into Scylla wishing to avoid Charybdis (adapted from Homer)
incipit	the beginning of a text
in commendam	in trust for a time
in contumaciam	in contempt of court
in corpore	in body or substance
incredulus odi	being skeptical I hate it (Horace)
in cruce spero	I hope in the Cross
incudi reddere	to return to the anvil (Horace)
in cumulo	in a heap
incunabula	earliest printed books, those before 1500
incunabulum	swaddling clothes; infancy; origin
in curia	in court
in custodia legis	in the custody of the law
inde irae et lacrimae	hence the anger and these tears (Juvenal)
in delicto	in fault, though not in equal fault
in Deo speramus	in God we hope (motto of Brown University)
in Deo speravi	in God have I trusted
in deposito	on deposit; as a pledge
Index Expurgatorius	list of books from which certain passages have been expurgated by the Catholic Church

Index Librorum Prohibitorum — list of books prohibited by the Catholic Church

index rerum — an index of matters

index verborum — an index of words

indicia — indications, signs and circumstances

indicium — indicating mark or sign

indictum sit — leave it unsaid

in diem vivere — to live for the day

in dies — daily, everyday

indignante invidia florebit iustus — the just man will flourish in spite of envy

in discrimine rerum — at the crisis point; at the turning point

indocilis pauperiem pati — one who cannot learn to bear poverty (Horace)

in dorso — on the back

in dubio — in doubt

in dulci jubilo — in sweet rejoicing

industriae nil impossibile — with hard work, nothing is impossible

inedita — unpublished compositions

in equilibrio — in equilibrium

in esse — in existence at the present time

inest clementia forti — clemency belongs to the bold

inest sua gratia parvis — trifles have a grace of their own

in excelsis — in the highest; to the greatest measure

in exitu — an issue

in extenso — in its entirety; completely

in extremis — at the point of death; at the extreme point

in facie curiae — in the presence of the court

in facto — in a state of completion

infandum, regina, iubes renovare dolorem — unspeakable, queen, is the grief which you wish me to renew (Virgil)

infandum renovare dolorem — to renew an unspeakable grief

infecta pace — without establishing peace (Terence)

in ferrum pro libertate ruebant — for freedom they rushed on their sword

in fieri — pending; not yet completed

infima species — the lowest species

infixum est mihi — I have firmly resolved

in flagrante delicto — while the crime is blazing

inflatilia — wind instruments

in folio — in the page

in forma pauperis — in the manner of a pauper; at no cost

in foro conscientiae — in the court of conscience

in foro domestico — in a domestic court

infra — below (in the text)

infra aetatem — under age, a minor

infra dignitatem (infra dig.) — beneath one's dignity

infra regnum — within the realm

in fumo — in smoke

in fusum — let it infuse

in futuro — in the future; at a later date

in genere	in kind; in the same class or species
ingenita levitas et erudita vanitas	frivolity is inborn, conceit is acquired by education (Cicero)
ingens aequor	the mighty ocean
ingens telum necessitatis	necessity is a powerful weapon
in gremio legis	in the lap of the law
in hac parte	on this part
in his verbis	in these (exact) words
in hoc	in this; respecting this matter
in hoc salus	there is safety
in hoc signo	by this sign (the Cross) (motto of the Jesuits)
in hoc signo spes mea	in this sign (the Cross) is my hope
in hoc signo vinces	by this sign you will conquer (moto of Constantine)
in infinitum	to infinity; forever
in intellectu	in intelligence; in conception
in invidium	against the unwilling; compulsory
in invitum	against the will of the other party
iniquia numquam regna perpetui manent	unjust rules never endure forever
iniquium est	it is inequitable or unjust
initio	at the beginning
iniuriae qui addideris contumeliam	you who have added insult to injury
in jure	according to law

injuria absque damno	a wrong without damage; insult without damage
injuria non excusat injuriam	one wrong does not justify another wrong
in limine	at the outset; on the threshold
in limine belli	at the outbreak of war (Livy)
in loco	in the place
in loco citato (loc. cit.)	occurring in the place cited
in loco parentis	in the place of a parent
in lumine tuo videbimus lumen	in thy light we shall see light (motto of Columbia University)
in malum partem	in a bad sense
in manus tuas commendo spiritum meum	into Thy hands I commend my spirit (Christ's final words on the Cross)
in maxima potentia, minima licentia	in the greatest power there is the least freedom
in medias res	in the middle of things
in medio	in the middle
in medio tutissimus ibis	you will go safest in the middle (Ovid)
in meditatione fugae	in contemplation of flight
in memoriam	in memory; document in memory of a person
in mora	in delay
in naturalibus	in a state of nature; naked
in nihil nil posse reverti	nothing cannot return to nothing (Persius)
in nocte consilium	in the night is counsel

in nomine	in the name of
in nomine Domini	in the name of the Lord
in nomine Patris et Filii et Spiritus Sancti	in the name of the Father and the Son and the Holy Spirit
in nubibus	in the clouds
in nuce	in a nutshell; in a concise manner
in oculis civium	in the eyes of the citizens
in omnia paratus	prepared for all things
in omnibus	in all things; in all respects
in omnibus caritas	in all things charity
inopem me copia fecit	abundance makes me poor (Ovid)
inopiae desunt multa, avaritiae omnia	poverty is the lack of many things, avarice of everything
in ovo	in the egg; immature
in pace	in peace
in pace, ut sapiens, apparat idonee bello	in peace, like a wise man, he appropriately prepares for war (Horace)
in pari causa	in an equal cause
in pari delicto	(two parties) in equal fault
in pari materia	regarding the same subject matter
in partibus infidelium	in the lands of infidels
in pectore	in the breast; in secret
in perpetuam rei memoriam	in perpetual remembrance
in perpetuum	forever; in perpetuity
in persona	in person

in personam	(a legal action) against the person
in plano	on a level surface
in pleno	in full; completely
in pontificalibus	in episcopal robes
in posse	as a possibility; potential action
in posterum	in the future
in potentia	in possibility
in praesentia	in the present; at the moment
in primis	among the first
in principio	in the beginning; at the outset
in procinctu	with girded loins
in promptu	in readiness
in propria causa	in one's own suit
in propria causa nemo iudex	no one can judge his own cause
in propria persona	in one's own person
in prospectu	in prospect
in puris naturalibus	in the natural state; naked
inquirendo	by inquiring
inquisitio post mortem	inquest after death
in re	in the matter of
in rem	(a legal action) against the thing
in rerum natura	in the nature of things
in saecula saeculorum	forever and ever; for ages and ages
insalutato hospite	leaving without thanking the host

insanus omnis furere credit ceteros	every madman thinks everyone else is mad (Syrus)
insculpsit	he or she engraved it
in se	in and of itself
in silvam ligna ferre	to carry wood to the forest
in situ	in the original place; usual environment
in solidum	in the whole
in solo Deo salus	in God alone there is salvation
in specie	in kind; in like form
instanter	urgently; immediately
instar omnium	worth all of them (Cicero)
in statu pupillari	having the status of a student
in statu quo	in the existing condition or situation
in statu quo ante	in the same condition as before
in statu quo ante bellum	in the condition before the war
institutiones	works containing elements of science
in tantum	in so much as
in te Domine, speravi	in Thee Lord, have I put my trust
integer vitae	living a blameless life (Horace)
integer vitae scelerisque purus	blameless in life and free from crime (Horace)
integra mens augustissima possessio	a sound and vigorous mind is the most honored possession

integros haurire fontes	to drink from pure fountains
intellectus agens	active intellect
intellectus merces est fidei	understanding is the reward of faith
intellectus possibilis	passive intellect
intelligenti pauca	to the intelligent, few words
in tempore opportuno	at the opportune time
in tenebris	in darkness; incomprehensible
inter	between, among
inter alia	among other things
inter alios	among other persons
inter arma leges silent	in time of wars, laws are silent
inter canem et lupum	between a dog and wolf
interdicere alicui aqua et igni	to forbid water and fire to someone (Cicero)
interdum volgus rectum videt, est ubi peccat	at times the world sees straight, but many times the world goes astray (Virgil)
inter malleum et incudem	between the hammer and the anvil
inter nos	among us, between us
inter pares	among peers; among those of equal rank
inter partes	with both parties represented
inter pocula	between cups; over drinks
inter regalia	among the festive activities
interregnum	the period between rulers

in terrorem	in fear; action based on extreme fear
inter se	among or between themselves
inter spem et metum	between hope and fear
inter vivos	between the living parties
interdum vulgus rectum videt	sometimes the crowd sees right (Horace)
in terminis	in express terms
in terrorem	as a warning
in testimonium	in witness
in totidem verbis	in so many words
in toto	as a whole, in its entirety
in toto caelo	in the whole sky
intra muros	within the walls
in transitu	in transit, in passage
intra parietes	within the walls
intra vires	within one's authority or jurisdiction
Introitus	the entrance (beginning of the Mass)
intuitu	in respect to, with regards to
intus et in cute novi hominem	I know the man within and in the skin
in usum Delphini	for the use of the Dauphin; expurgated
in utero	in the womb
in utroque fidelis	faithful in both
in utroque iure	under both laws (civil and canon)
in utrumque paratus	prepared for either alternative (Virgil)
in vacuo	in space; isolated

invadio	in pledge
invenit	he or she devised it
in ventre	in the womb
in verba peccare	to offend in words only
inverso ordine	in inverse order
invictus maneo	I remain unconquered
in vino veritas	in wine, there is truth
invita Minerva	Minerva was unwilling; uninspired
in vitro	in glass; in a culture dish
invitium sequitur honor	honor follows him uninvited
in vivo	in the living organism
Ioannes est nomen eius	John is his name (Motto of Puerto Rico)
ioci causa	for the sake of a joke
io Triumphe	hail, god of Triumph
ipsa quidem pretium virtus sibi	virtue is its own reward (Claudian)
ipsa scientia potestas est	knowledge itself is power (Francis Bacon)
ipse dixit	he himself said it; unsubstantiated assertion
ipsissima verba	quoted in the exact words
ipso facto	by the fact itself
ipso jure	by the law itself
ira furor brevis est	anger is brief madness (Horace)
irae et lacrimae	resentment and tears
irrevocabile verbum	a word beyond recall
irritabis crabrones	you will stir up the hornets
ita est	it is so

ita lex scripta est	thus is written the law
ita te Deus adiuvet	so help you God
italice	in the Italian manner
ite missa est	go, the Mass has ended
item	also, likewise
iterum	again, anew
Iubilate Deo	rejoice in God
iucundi acti labores	past labors are pleasant (Cicero)
iudicium Dei	the judgment of God
iudicium parium aut leges terrae	the judgment of one's peers are the laws of the land (from the Magna Charta)
iuncta iuvant	united things help each other
iuncta iuvant, alta petit	union is strength, it seeks the heights
iuniores ad labores	the younger men for labor
Iuppiter Tonans	Jupiter the Thunderer
iura naturae sunt immutabilia	the laws of nature are unchangeable
iura regalia	royal rights
iurare in verba a magistri	to swear to the words of the master (Horace)
iurat	he or she swears
iure	by one's right
iure belli	by the right of war
iure coronae	by the right of the crown
iure divino	by divine right
iure gentium	by the right of nations
iure humano	by human law
iure mariti	by the husband's right

iure non dono	by right, not gift
iure propinquitatis	by right of relationship
iure sanguinis	by right of blood
iure uxoris	the right of the wife
iurisdictionis fundandae causa	for the sake of establishing jurisdiction
iuris ignorantia est cum nostrum ignoramus	in the ignorance of the laws, we are unfamiliar with our own rights
iuris peritus	learned in the law
iuris praecepta	the precepts of law
Iuris Utriusque Doctor	Doctor of Both Laws (civil and canon)
ius	law, legal right
ius accrescendi	the right of survivors
ius canonicum	canon law
ius civile	civil law
ius civitatis	right of citizens
ius commune	common law
ius contra bellum	law against war
ius divinum	divine law
ius est ars boni et aequi	law is the art of the good and the just
ius et norma loquendi	the law and rule of speech
ius ex iniuria non oritur	right does not rise out of wrong
ius gentium	the law of nations
ius gladii	the right of the sword
ius in bello	moral constraints in war
ius in re	an actual right
iusiurandum	a swearing; an oath
ius mariti	the right of the husband
ius naturae	the law of nature

ius non scriptum	unwritten law
ius pignoris	the right of pledge
ius possessionis	the right of possession
ius postliminii	the right of resumption of status
ius primae noctis	the right of first night
ius proprietatis	the right of property
ius regium	the right of the crown
ius relictae	the right of the widow
ius sanguinis	the law of consanguinity
ius scriptum	written law; statutory
ius soli	the law of birthplace
ius summum, saepe summa malitia est	extreme law is often an extreme wrong (Terence)
ius tertii	the rights of the third party
iustitiae soror fides	faith is the sister of justice
iustitiae tenax	tenacious of justice
iustitia omnibus	justice for all (motto of the District of Columbia)
iusto tempore	at the proper time
iustum et tenax propositi vir	a man who is upright and steadfast in purpose (Horace)
iuvante Deo	God helping

L

labitur et labetur in omne — (the stream) flows and it will flow forever (Horace)

laborare est orare — to work is to pray

labore et honore — by labor and honor

labor ipse voluptas — work itself is a pleasure (Manilus)

labor omnia vincit — work conquers all things (motto of Oklahoma)

labor omnia vincit improbus — persistent work conquers all things (Virgil)

labor optimos citat — labor summons the best men (Seneca)

laborum dulce lenimen — sweet solace of (my) labor (Horace)

labuntur et imputantur — (the moments) slip away and are reckoned to our account (inscription on a sundial)

lacrima Christi — the tear of Christ; also a sweet Italian wine

lacrimae rerum — tears for the things; pity for misfortune

lacrimis oculos suffusa nitentes — her sparkling eyes suffused with tears (Virgil)

lacuna — gap, blank space, hiatus

laesa majestas — the crime of high treason

laevus — left; left-handed

lana caprina — goat's wool; an imaginary thing

lapis	stone
lapis philosophorum	the philosophers' stone
lapsus	slip; blunder
lapsus calami	slip of the pen
lapsus linguae	slip of the tongue
lapsus memoriae	lapse of memory
lapsus morum	slip of morals
lapsus pennae	slip of the pen
lararium	shrine for images of the lares
lares et penates	Roman gods of the household
lar familiaris	domestic or household spirit
lateat scintillula forsan	perhaps a spark may exist unseen
latet anguis in herba	a snake lies hidden in the grass
lato sensu	in a broad sense
laudandum adulescentem, ornandum, tollendum	let's praise the young man, honor him, and elevate him (Cicero on Octavian)
laudari a laudato viro	to be praised by a man who is praised (Cicero)
laudator temporis acti	one who praises past times (Horace)
laudem virtutis necessitati damus	we give to necessity the praise of virtue (Quintilian)
laus Deo	praise be to God
laus propria sordet	self-praise is base
lectio difficilior	the harder reading; principle of selection

lector benevole
kind reader; opening of an author's preface

legalis homo
a legal man; a man with full rights

legatus a latere
ambassador from inner circle; papal legate

legenda
things to be read

lege, quaeso
read, I pray you

leges bonae ex malis moribus procreantur
good laws are the products of bad morals

leges mori serviunt
laws are servants to custom

legimus, ne legantur
we read so that others may not read (Lactantius)

leone fortior fides
faith is stronger than a lion

leonina societas
a leonine partnership, one in which one partner shares the losses but not the profits

lex
the law

lex domicilii
the law in force at one's domicile

lex est dictamen rationis
law is the dictate of reason

lex loci
the law of the place

lex loci contractus
the legal place of making a contract

lex loci delicti
the location where a wrong took place

lex, lux
law, light (motto of Emory University)

lex mercatorum
law merchant; mercantile law

lex non scripta
unwritten law; common law; customary law

lex Salica	Salic law (females cannot inherit the throne)
lex scripta	written law, statutory law
lex talionis	the law of retribution or retaliation
lex terrae	the law of the land
libelli divortii	document of divorce
libelli famosi	defamatory publication
libellus rerum	book of things; an inventory
libellus supplex	book of supplies; requisition
libera arbitria	free decisions
liberavi animam meam	I have freed my mind
liber evangeliorum	book of Gospels
liber judiciarum	book of judgment
libertas inestimabilis res est	freedom is a possession of profound value
liberum arbitrium	freedom of choice
liberum arbitrium indifferentiae	freedom of indifference; ability to choose without reference to antecedent
liberum voluntatis arbitrium	free choice of the will
librae, solidi, denarii	pounds, shillings, pence
licentia vatum	the license of poets
licet	it is allowed
ligna et lapides	sticks and stones
lignum vitae	wood of life; a tropical tree
ligonem ligonem vocat	he calls a hoe a hoe (a spade a spade)
limae labor et mora	the toil and delay of the snail (Horace)

limbus	paradise; limbo
limbus fatuorum	fools' paradise
limbus infantium	infants' paradise
limbus patrum	fathers' paradise
limbus puerorum	children's paradise
linea recta	straight line
lingua franca	mixture of languages
lingua romanica	Latin of the Dark Ages
linguae verbera	the tongue's lashings
lis litem generat	litigation engenders litigation
lis pendens	a suspended lawsuit
lis sub judice	a lawsuit before the judge
litem lite resolvere	to settle a dispute with litigation
lite pendente	while the lawsuit is pending
litterati	men of learning; the learned class
litteratim	letter for letter
littera scripta manet	the written letter abides
litterae humaniores	the humanities; the human letters
litterae scriptae	written letters; manuscript
litterae sine moribus vanae	literature without character is vain (motto of the University of Pennsylvania)
loco	in the place
loco citato (loc. cit.)	in the place cited
loco laudato	in the place cited with approval
loco supra citato	in the place cited before

locum tenens	one holding the place; a substitute
locus	a place; written passage
locus citatus	the passage cited
locus classicus	standard source of an idea or reference
locus communis	a commonplace passage; a public place
locus criminis	the place of the crime
locus delicti	the place of the crime
locus in quo	the place at which an action took place
locus poenitentiae	a place for repentance
locus sigilli (L.S.)	the place of the seal (on a contract)
locus standi	a place to stand; recognized position
longe aberrat scopo	he wanders far from the objective
longe absit	far be it from me
longo intervallo	at a long interval
longo sed proximus intervallo	the next, but after a long interval (Virgil)
loquitur	he or she speaks
lubricum linguae	slip of the tongue
luce lucet aliena	it shines with another's light
lucernam olet	it smells of the lamp
lucidus ordo	a clear arrangement (Horace)
lucri causa	for the sake of gain
lucri bonus est odor ex re qualibet	sweet is the smell of money obtained from any source (Juvenal)

lucus a non lucendo	called a grove from the absence of light; a paradoxical explanation
ludere cum sacris	to play with sacred things
lues	a plague; pestilence
lumen	light
lumen fidei	light of faith
lumen gratiae	light of grace
lumenque iuventae purpureum	the purple light of youth (Virgil)
lupum auribus tenere	to hold a wolf by the ears
lupus est homo homini	man is wolf to man (Plautus)
lupus in fabula	the wolf in the fable (Terence)
lupus pilum mutat, non mentem	the wolf changes his coat, not his mind
lusus naturae	freak of nature; an unusual occurrence
lustrum	a period of five years
lux	light
lux aeterna	eternal light
lux benigna	kindly light
lux est umbra Dei	light is the shadow of God (Symonds)
lux et lex	light and law (motto of the University of North Dakota)
lux et veritas	light and truth (motto of Yale University)
lux, libertas	light, liberty (motto of the University of North Carolina at Chapel Hill)
lux mundi	light of the world
lux venit ab alto	light comes from above

M

macte	bravo: well-done
macte animo	be increased in courage; be brave
macte virtute	be increased by merit; prosper
magis mutus quam piscis	quieter than a fish
magister	master
magister artis ingeniique largitor venter	the stomach is the teacher of art and the bestower of genius (Persius)
Magister Artium	Master of Arts
magister ceremoniarum	master of ceremonies
magister dixit	the master has spoken (reference to Aristotle)
magister ludi	master of public games; a schoolteacher
magister rerum usus	use is the master of things
magistra rerum experientia	experience is the mistress of things
magistratus indicat virum	the office shows the man
Magna Charta	the Great Charter of 1215, granted by King John
magna Christi	the great works of Christ
magna civitas, magna solitudo	a great city, a great solitude

magna cum laude	with high honors; with great distinction
magna di curant, parva neglegunt	the gods attend to great matters, they neglect the small ones (Cicero)
magna est veritas	great is the truth
magna est veritas et praevalet	great is the truth and it prevails
magna est vis consuetudinis	great is the force of habit (Cicero)
magna servitus est magna fortuna	a great fortune is a great slavery (Seneca)
magnae spes altera Romae	another hope for Rome (refers to Ascanius)
magnas inter opes inops	poor in the midst of great riches (Horace)
magnificat anima mea Dominum	my soul magnifies the Lord (Gospel of Luke)
magni nominis umbra	under the shadow of a great name (Lucan)
magni pectoris est inter secunda moderatio	moderation in prosperity is the mark of a great heart (Livy)
magno conatu magnas nugas	by great effort (one obtains) great trifles (Terence)
magnos homines virtute metimur, non fortuna	we measure great men by their virtue, not by their fortune
magnum bonum	a great good
magnum in parvo	great things in small things
magnum opus	most important work of writer or artist (pl. magna)

magnum vectigal est parsimonia	economy is a great revenue (Cicero)
magnus ab integro saeculonum	the great cycle of the ages is born again (Virgil)
major e longinquo reverentia	greater reverence from a distance
majores pennas nido	wings greater than the nest (Horace)
majusculae	large or capital letters
mala fide	in bad faith
mala fides	bad faith
male facere qui vult numquam non causam invenit	those who intend to do evil never fail to find a reason
maleficium	an evil deed, a crime
male parta male dilabuntur	things obtained by evil are lost by evil (Cicero)
malesuada fames	desire that leads to a crime (Virgil)
male verum examinat omnis corruptus iudex	a corrupt judge weighs truth in false scales (Horace)
mali exempli	of a bad example; of a bad precedent
malignum spernere vulgus	to scorn the evil crowd (Horace)
mali principii malus finis	the bad end of a bad beginning
malis avibus	under unfavorable signs; inauspicious
malitia praecogitata	malice aforethought
malo animo	with evil intent
malo grato	in spite; unwilling
malo in consilio feminae vincunt viros	women surpass men in scheming evil deeds

malo modo	in an evil manner
malo mori quam foedari	I would rather die than be dishonored
malum	an evil; a wrong
malum in se	wrong in itself
malum prohibitum	wrong because it is prohibited by statute
malus pudor	false shame
mandamus	we command; writ commanding performance
mane	morning
mane primo	first thing in the morning
manet	he or she remains
manet alta mente repositum	it remains stored deep in the mind (Virgil)
manet cicatrix	the scar remains
mane et nocte	morning and night
mania a potu	mania from drinking; delirium tremens
manibus pedibusque	with hands and feet; with total devotion
manifesta probatione non indigent	manifest things do not require proof
manu forti	with a strong hand; by force
manu propria	with one's own hand
manus nubibus	a hand from the clouds
manus haec inimica tyrannis	this hand is enemy to the tyrants
mare clausum	closed sea, under jurisdiction of one state
mare liberum	an open sea, not subject to jurisdiction

mare nostrum	our sea (the Mediterranean)
margaritas ante porcos	pearls before swine (Gospel of Matthew)
marginalia	notes in the margin; of trifling importance
Mars gravior sub pace latet	a harsher war lies hidden under peace
martyres non facit poena sed causa	the cause and not the punishment makes the martyr (St. Augustine)
mater	mother
mater artium necessitas	necessity is the mother of arts
Mater Dolorosa	a sorrowful mother (the Virgin Mary)
materfamilias	female head of the family
materia medica	substances used as medicine
materiam superabat opus	the work surpassed the material (Ovid)
mater timidi flere non raro	the mother of a careful man seldom has reason to weep
matre pulchra, filia pulchrior	a daughter more beautiful than her mother (Horace)
matrix ecclesia	mother church
maturato opus est	there is need for haste (Livy)
maxima cum laude	with highest honors; with greatest distinction
maxima debetur puero reverentia	the greatest respect is due a child (Juvenal)

maximae cuique fortunae minime credendum est — the greatest good fortune is the least to be trusted (Livy)

maximus in minimus — great things in small things; less is more

mea culpa — my fault; I am guilty; admission of guilt

mea maxima culpa — through my very great fault

mea mihi conscientia pluris est quam omnium sermo — my own conscience is more to me than what the world says (Cicero)

mea virtute me involvo — I wrap myself with my virtue (Horace)

media in vitae in morte sumus — in the midst of life we are in death

medice, cura te ipsum — physician, heal thyself (Gospel of Luke)

medicus enim nihil aliud est quam animi consolatio — a doctor is nothing but someone to ease the conscience (Petronius)

medii aevi — of the Middle Ages

mediocria firma — the middle course is most secure

medio tutissimus ibis — you will go safest in the middle (Ovid)

meditatio fugae — contemplation of flight

medium tenere beati — happy are those who keep a middle course

me judice — in my judgment; in my opinion

meliores priores — the better, the first

melioribus annis — in the better years (Virgil)

melius est omnia mala pati quam malo consentire — it is better to suffer every evil than to consent to evil

membra disjecta	scattered limbs; scattered fragments
memento homo, quia pulvis es et in pulverem revertis	remember man, that dust thou art and to dust thou shalt return (Genesis)
memento mori	reminder of death
memorabilia	things worth remembering
memor et fidelis	mindful and faithful
memoria in aeterna	in everlasting remembrance
memoria technica	system or device to assist the memory
memoriter	from memory; memorized by heart
mendacem memorem esse oportet	it is fitting that a liar have a good memory (Quintilian)
mens aequa in arduis	a calm mind in difficult situations (Horace)
mensa et toro	from bed and board
mens agitat molem	the mind moves matter (Virgil)
mens conscia recti	mind conscious of righteousness
mens divinior	an inspired mind (Horace)
mens invicta manet	the mind remains unconquered
mens legis	the spirit of the law
mens rea	guilty mind; condition necessary for a crime
mens sana in corpore sano	a healthy mind in a healthy body (Juvenal)

mens sibi conscia recti	a mind conscious to itself of righteousness; a good conscience (Virgil)
mentis gratissimus error	a very delightful apparition (Horace)
meo periculo	at my risk
meos tam suspicione quam crimine iudico carere oportere	members of my family should never be suspected of breaking the law (Caesar)
meo voto	by my wish
meret qui laborat	he who works is deserving
meridie	in the middle of the day; at noon
merum sal	pure salt; Attic wit
metiri se quemque suo modulo ac pede verum cst	the true course is that each should measure himself with his own yardstick (Horace)
meum et teum	mine and yours
mihi cura futuri	my care is for the future
miles gloriosus	a boastful soldier
militat omnis amans	every lover serves as a soldier (Ovid)
militiae species amor est	love is a type of military service (Ovid)
minatur innocentibus qui parcit nocentibus	he threatens the innocent who spares the guilty
minima de malis	of the evils, (choose) the least
minusculae	small Roman letters
mirabile dictu	wonderful to relate
mirabile visu	wonderful to behold
mirabilia	wonders, miracles

mirum in modum	in a wonderful manner (Caesar)
mirum videtur quod sit factum iam diu	it appears marvelous because it was done long ago
miscebis sacra profanis	you will mix sacred things with profane (Horace)
misce stultitiam consiliis brevem	mix some foolishness with your wisdom (Horace)
miserabile dictu	sad to relate
miserabile vulgus	the wretched mob
miseranda vita, qui se metui, quam amari malunt	pitiable is the life of those who prefer to be feared rather than to be loved
Miserere mei	have mercy on me (Psalm 51)
miserere nobis	have mercy on us
misericordia	a plea to have mercy
Misericordia Domini	God's mercy
Misericordias Domine	God have mercy on us
miseris succurrere disco	I learn to help the sad ones (Virgil)
Missa	the Mass
Missa bassa	Low Mass
Missa cantata	sung Mass
Missa catechumenorum	Mass of the catechumens
Missa fedelium	Mass of the faithful
Missa solemnis	High Mass
mitis sapientia	ripe wisdom
mitius imperanti melius paretur	the more mildly one commands, the better one is obeyed

mitte decem tales	send ten like this
mittimus	we send; writ to commit person to prison
mobile perpetuum	something in perpetual motion
mobile vulgus	the fickle crowd
moderandum inculpatae tutelae	the regulation of justifiable defense
moderata durant	things used in moderation endure
modo et forma	in manner and form
modo praescripto	in the manner written
modulus	measure of relative size
modus	mode; manner; method
modus docendi	method of teaching
modus loquendi	method of speaking; style of speech
modus operandi	method of operation
modus ponens	constructive hypothetical syllogism
modus tenendi	manner of holding
modus tollens	destructive hypothetical syllogism
modus vivendi	mode of living together
mole ruit sua	it falls down of its own weight (Horace)
mollia tempora	favorable times
mollia tempora fandi	favorable times for speaking
mollissima fandi tempora	the most favorable time for speaking (Virgil)
montani semper liberi	mountaineers are always free men (motto of West Virginia)

monumentum aere perennius	a monument more lasting than bronze (Horace)
more	in the manner of
more Anglico	in the English fashion
more dicto	in the manner directed
more Hibernico	in the Irish fashion
more majorum	in the manner of our ancestors
more meo	in my own fashion
more Socratico	in the manner of Socrates
more solito	in the usual manner
more suo	in his own manner
mores	customs, habits, traditions, manners
moribus antiquis res stat Romana virisque	the Roman people stand on ancient heroes and ancient customs
morituri morituros salutant	those who are about to die salute
morituri te salutamus	we who are about to die salute you
mors beneficia	kindly death
mors et vita	death and life
mors ianua vitae	death is the gate of life
mors omnia solvit	death dissolves all things
mors omnibus communis	death is common to all men
mors tua, vita mea	you must die so that I may live
mors ultima linea rerum est	death is the final goal of things (Horace)
mortalium rerum misera beatitudo	the wretched happiness of mortal things
mortis causa	because of death; anticipating death

mortui non mordent	dead men don't bite
mortuo leoni et lepores insultant	even hares leap on a dead lion
mortuus sine prole	dead without children
mos maiorum	the custom of one's ancestors
mos pro lege	custom for law
motu proprio	of one's own impulse, one's own initiative
mox nox in rem	soon night, (let's get down) to the business
muliebre ingenium, prolubium, occasio	a woman's nature is desire, opportunity
multa acervatim frequentans	crowding together many thoughts (Cicero)
multa docet fames	hunger teaches us many things
multa fidem promissa levant	many promises lessen faith (Horace)
multa gemens	with many groans
multi multa, nemo omnia novit	many have known much, but no one has known everything
multa paucis	much in few words
multa petentibus desunt multa	to those who desire many things, many things are lacking (Horace)
multa tulit fecitque	he has suffered and done much (Horace)
multo enim multoque quam hostem superare operosius	it is harder to conquer oneself than to conquer one's enemy
multos experimus ingratos, plures facimus	many men are ungrateful, but more we make ungrateful (Seneca)

multi sunt vocati, pauci vero electi	many are called, but few are chosen (Gospel of Matthew)
multum demissus homo	a very modest man (Horace)
multum in parvo	much in little
multum, non multa	much, not many (Pliny the Elder)
munditiis capimur	we are captivated by neatness (Ovid)
mundus	the world
mundus intelligibilis	the world of intelligible realities
mundus sensibilis	the world of things perceived by the senses
mundus vult decipi	the world wants to be deceived
Munera Pulveris	Gifts of the Dust (Horace)
munus Apolline dignum	a gift worthy of Apollo (Horace)
murus aeneus conscientia sana	a sound conscience is a wall of brass
muscae volantes	flying flies; specks before the eyes
mutanda	things to be changed
mutare vel timere sperno	I hate to change or fear
mutatio nominis	a change of name
mutatis mutandis	after making the necessary changes
mutato nomine	the name being changed
mutato nomine de te fabula narratur	with the names changed, the story applies to you (Horace)
mutum est pictura poema	the picture is a silent poem
mutuus consensus	mutual consent

N

nam et ipsa scientia potestas est

for knowledge is itself power (Francis Bacon)

nam tua res agitur, paries cum proximus ardet

when your neighbor's house is on fire, you are in danger yourself (Horace)

nascentes morimur

from birth we begin to die (Manilius)

nascimur poetae, fimus oratores

we are born poets, we are made orators

natale solum

native soil

natio comoeda est

it is a nation of comics (Juvenal)

natura abhorret vacuum

nature abhors a vacuum (Descartes)

natura appetit perfectum

nature covets perfection

naturam expelles furca tamen usque recurret

you may drive nature out with a pitchfork, but it will still return (Horace)

natura naturans

nature naturing; scholastic term for manifestation of God

natura naturata

nature natured; created things of the world

natura non facit saltum

nature makes no leaps; nature is consistent

natura vero nihil hominibus brevitate vitae praestitit melius	nature has granted man no better gift than the brevity of life
natus ad gloriam	born to glory
natus nemo	not a born soul (Plautus)
ne admittas	do not admit
nec Aesopum quidem trivit	he has not even gone through Aesop
nec amor nec tussis celatur	neither love nor a cough can be hidden
nec aspera terrent	not even difficulties deter us
nec caput nec pedes	neither head nor tail; utter confusion
nec cupias nec metuas	neither desire nor fear
nec deus intersit, nisi dignus vindice nodus inciderit	neither should a god intervene unless a knot befalls worthy of his interference
ne cede malis	do not yield to misfortune
ne cede malis, sed contra audientior	do not yield to misfortunes, but go forth more boldly to meet them (Virgil)
necesse est aut imiteris aut oderis	you must either imitate or loathe the world (Seneca)
necesse est multos timeat quem multi timent	he must fear many, whom many fear (Caesar)
necessitas non habet legem	necessity has no law
nec habeo, nec careo, nec curo	I have not, I want not, I care not
nec male notus eques	a well-known knight
nec mora nec requies	neither delay nor rest

nec placida contentus quiete est	nor is he content with peaceful repose
nec pluribus impar	not unequal to most (motto of Louis XIV)
nec prece nec pretio	neither by entreaty nor by bribe
nec quaerere nec spernere honorem	neither to seek nor to despise honors
nec semper feriet quodcumque minabitur arcus	nor will the bow always hit what it threatens to hit (Horace)
nec scire fas est omnia	nor is it permitted to know everything
nec tecum possum vivere, nec sine te	I can neither live with you, nor without you (Martial)
nec temere nec timide	neither rashly nor timidly
nec timeo nec sperno	I neither fear nor despise
nec vitia nostra nec remedia pati possumus	we can endure neither our vices nor the remedy for them (Livy)
nec vixit male, qui natus moriensque fefellit	he has not lived badly who has been born and died without notice (Horace)
ne exeat regno	do not let him go out of the realm
nefasti dies	the legal holidays
ne fronti crede	trust not in appearances
negatur	it is denied
negotium populo romano melius quam otium committi	Romans understand work better than leisure
ne Iuppiter quidem omnibus placet	not even Jupiter himself can please everyone
nemo alius	no one else

nemo bis punitur pro eodem delicto	no man is punished twice for the same crime
nemo cogitationis poenam patitur	no one is punished for his thoughts
nemo dat quod non habet	no one can give what he does not have
nemo enim est tam senex qui se annum non putet posse vivere	no one is so old as to think that he cannot live more years (Cicero)
nemo est heres viventis	no one is heir to a living man
nemo est supra leges	nobody is above the law
nemo liber est qui corpori servit	no one is free who is a slave to his body
nemo malus felix	no bad man is happy
nemo me impune lacessit	no one provokes me with impunity (motto of the kings ot Scotland)
nemo mortalium omnibus horis sapit	no mortal is wise at all times (Pliny the Elder)
ne moveas Camarinam	don't disturb Camarina; let well enough alone
nemo repente fuit turpissimus	no one becomes very wicked suddenly (Juvenal)
nemo risum praebuit qui ex se cepit	no one becomes a fool who laughs at himself
nemo silens placuit, multi brevitate loquendi	no one pleases by silence, many please by brevity of speech
nemo solus satis sapit	one is wise enough by himself (Plautus)
ne nimium	not too much; nothing in excess
ne obliviscaris	lest you forget

ne pereant lege mane rosas, cito virgo senescit pick roses in the morning lest they fade; a maiden soon grows old

ne plus ultra nothing more beyond; the highest point

ne puero gladium (don't give) a sword to a boy

neque femina amissa pudicitia alia abnuerit a woman after losing her virtue will hesitate at nothing (Tacitus)

neque semper arcum tendit Apollo Apollo does not always keep a bent bow (Horace)

ne quid nimis nothing in excess

nervi belli pecunia infinita plenty of money is the muscle of war

nervus probandi the sinew of proof; the primary argument

nervus rerum the sinew of things; the major things

nescio quid I know not what

nescit vox missa reverti a word once spoken can never be recalled (Horace)

ne supra crepidam sutor iudicaret the cobbler should not judge above the sandal (Pliny the Elder)

ne sutor supra crepidam let not the cobbler judge above the sandal

ne tradas sine nummo do not deliver without money

Ne Temere not rashly; a Roman Catholic decree declaring a marriage invalid

ne tentes, aut perfice accomplish or do not attempt

niger cygnus	a black swan; an unusual person
nigro notanda lapillo	to mark with a black stone
nihil	nothing
nihil ad rem	nothing to the matter; irrelevant issue
nihil agendo homines male agere discunt	by doing nothing, man learns to act wickedly
nihil amori iniuriam est	there is no injury that love won't forgive
nihil debet	he owes nothing
nihil dicit	he says nothing
nihil est ab omni parte beatum	nothing is blessed in every respect
nihil est aliud falsitas nisi veritatis imitatio	the false is nothing but an imitation of the truth
nihil est miserum nisi quum putes	nothing is wretched unless you think so
nihil ex nihilo	nothing from nothing
nihil ex nihilo fit	nothing comes from nothing
nihil interit	nothing dies
nihil obstat quo minus imprimatu	nothing hinders it from being published
nihil obstat	nothing hinders; nothing withstanding
nihil peccat nisi quod nihil peccat	his only fault is that he has no faults
nihil quod tetigit non ornavit	he touched nothing that he did not adorn
nihil novi sub sole	there is nothing new under the sun

nihil tam munitum quod non expugnari pecunia possit
no place is so strongly fortified that money could not capture it (Cicero)

nil admirari
to be excited about nothing (Horace)

nil agit exemplum, litem quod lite resolvit
resolving one litigation by creating another does not serve as an example (Horace)

nil conscire sibi, nulla pallescere culpa
to be conscious of no wrongdoing, to turn pale at no crime (Horace)

nil consuetudine maius
nothing is greater than custom

nil desperandum
do not despair; no reason to despair (Horace)

nil dicit
he says nothing

nil ego contulerim iucundo sanus amico
never while I keep my senses shall I compare anything to the delight of a friend (Horace)

nil est amore veritatis celsius
nothing is more sublime than love of truth

nil fuit umquam sic impar sibi
nothing was ever so inconsistent with itself

nil homine terra peius ingrato creat
the earth produces nothing worse than an ungrateful man

nil igitur fieri de nilo posse fatendum
therefore we must state that nothing comes from nothing (Lucretius)

nil ligatum
nothing bound; without obligation

nil magnum nisi bonum
nothing is great unless good

nil mihi rescribas, tu tamen ipse veni	write nothing back to me, come yourself (Ovid)
nil mortalibus arduum est	nothing is too difficult for mortals (Horace)
nil nisi bonum	(say) nothing unless good
nil nisi Cruce	nothing unless by the Cross
nil non mortale tenemus, pectoris exceptis ingeniique bonis	we possess nothing that is not mortal except the blessings of heart and mind
nil novi sub sole	nothing new under the sun (Ecclesiastes)
nil obstat tibi, dum ne sit te ditior alter	nothing stops you, if only there may be no rival richer than yourself
nil posse creari de nilo	nothing can be created out of nothing
nil sine Deo	nothing without God
nil sine magno vita labore dedit mortalibus	the prizes of life are never to be had without trouble
nil sine numine	nothing without divine will (motto of Colorado)
nil ultra	nothing beyond
nimium ne crede colori	do not trust in a pleasing complexion (Virgil)
nisi	unless; coming into effect at the latest time
nisi Dominus frustra	unless the Lord (builds the house) in vain
nisi prius	unless the first; unless the original (legal doctrine)

nitor in adversum	I go forth against the opposite side (Ovid)
nobilitas sola est atque unica virtus	virtue is the only true nobility (Juvenal)
nobilitatis virtus non stemma character	virtue, not blood, is the mark of nobility
nocet empta dolore voluptas	pleasures bought by pain are harmful (Horace)
nocte	night
nocte et mane	night and morning
nolens volens	whether willing or unwilling
noli irritare leones	do not stir up the lions
noli me tangere	touch me not (Christ to Mary Magdalene)
nolle prosequi	prosecutor does not wish to continue
nolo contendere	I do not wish to contend a defense
nolo episcopari	I do not wish to serve (a public office)
nomen	name
nomen atque omen	a name and an omen (Plautus)
nomen genericum	a generic name
nomen nudum	a naked name
nomen specificum	a specific name
nomina stultorum parietibus haerent	the names of fools stick on the walls
nominis umbra	the shadow of a name
non Angli, se angeli	not Angles, but angels (Pope Gregory)
non assumpsit	he does not undertake
non bis in idem	not twice for the same thing

non causa pro causa	no cause for cause; a logical fallacy
non compos mentis	not in control of one's mind
non constat	it does not appear
non cuivis homini contingit adire Corinthum	it is not allowed that every man go to Corinth (Horace)
non datur ad musas currere lata via	there is no royal road to Art
non datur tertium	no third (choice) is given
non deficiente crumena	the purse not failing (Horace)
nondum editus	not yet published
nondum victoria, iam discordia erat	victory is almost at hand, but dissension has already begun
non erat his locus	that was not the place for these things
nones	nine days before the ides of the month on the ancient Roman calendar
non esse	not to be; nonexistence
non est	he or she is not
non est ad astra mollis e terris via	there is no easy way to the stars from earth (Seneca)
non est factum	it is not done; not bound to a contract
non est inventus	(the person) could not be found
non est iocus esse malignum	there is no joke where there's malice (Horace)
non est meus actus	it is not my act
non est tanti	it is not of such great importance

non est vivere sed valere vita est

life is not only being alive, but being well (Martial)

non generant aquilae columbas

eagles do not bear doves

non grata

not acceptable, not welcome

non ignarus mali, miseris succurrere disco

no stranger to misfortune myself, I learn to relieve the suffering of others (Virgil)

non inferiora secutus

not having followed anything inferior (Virgil)

non libet

it does not please me

non licet omnibus adire Corinthum

not everyone is allowed to go to Corinth (Horace)

non liquet

it is not clear

non mihi, non tibi, sed nobis

not for you, not for me, but for us both

non mihi, sed Deo et regi

not for myself, but for God and the king

non ministrari, sed ministrare

not to be administered to, but to administer

non multa, sed multum

not many things, but much

non nobis

not unto us

non nobis Domine

not unto us Lord (Psalm 115)

non nobis solum nati sumus

not only for ourselves are we born (Cicero)

non nostrum inter vos tantas componere lites

it is not for me to settle such serious controversies between you (Virgil)

non nova sed nove	not new things but in a new manner
non obstante	notwithstanding
non obstante veredicto	notwithstanding the verdict
non olet	it does not smell
non omne licitum honestum	not every lawful thing is honorable
non omne quod licet honestum est	what is pemissible is not always honorable
non omnia possumus omnes	we cannot all do everything (Virgil)
non omnis moriar	I shall not die entirely (Horace)
non passibus aequis	not with equal steps (Virgil)
non placet	it does not please; to give a negative vote
non possidentem multa vocaveris recte beatum	you cannot properly call happy the man who has many things (Horace)
non possumus	we are not able (to act on the matter)
non potest amor cum timore misceri	love and fear exclude each other
non prosequitur	he has not proceeded in the action
non qui parum habet, sed qui plus cupit, pauper est	it is not the man who has little, but the man who wants more, who is poor
non quis sed quid	not who but what
non quo sed quando	not by whom but when
non repetatur	let it not be repeated
non revertar inultus	I shall not return unavenged

non satis est puris versum perscribere verbis	it is not enough to make up your verse of plain words (Horace)
non semper ea sunt quae videntur	things are never what they seem
non semper erit aestas	it will not always be summer
non semper Saturnalia erunt	it will not always be Saturnalia
non semper temeritas est felix	temerity is not always successful (Livy)
non sequitur	it does not follow; not in logical succession
non sibi sed omnibus	not for himself but for all
non sibi sed patriae	not for himself but for his country
non sine numine	not without divine aid
non subito delenda	things not to be suddenly destroyed
non sum qualis eram	I am not the sort of person I was (Horace)
non sum qualis eram bonae sub regno Cinarae	I am not the person I was under the reign of good Cynara (Horace)
non sui juris	not by his own authority or legal right
non tali auxilio	not for such aid as this (Virgil)
non teneas aurum totum quod splendet ut aurum	do not take as gold everything that shines like gold
nonum prematur in annum	let it be kept back from publication until the ninth year (Horace)
non ut edam vivo, sed ut vivam edo	I do not live to eat, but eat to live

non veniunt in idem pudor atque amor	modesty and love are not at one (Ovid)
non vobis solum	not for you alone
non vult contendere	he does not wish to contest the charge
norma agendi	rule for conduct
nosce te ipsum	know thyself (Plutarch)
nosce tempus	know thy time
noscitur a sociis	he is known by his associates
nos duo turba sumus	we two are a crowd (Ovid)
nostro periculo	at our own risk
nostrum	our own; a patent medicine
nota bene	note well; take notice
notandum	something to be noted
nota notae est nota rei ipsius	a known component of a thing is known by the thing itself
notatu dignum	worthy of note
notiones communes	common notions
nova patria	a new country
novena	nine days' devotion
noverint universi per praesentes	they know all men by those present
novissima verba	the final words
novus homo	a new man; a parvenu
novus rex, nova lex	a new king, a new law
novus ordo seclorum	a new order of the ages (motto on the Great Seal of the United States)
nuda verba	naked words; plain words
nuda veritas	the naked truth

nudum pactum — a bare contract; merely a promise

nudus amor formae non amat artificem — cupid is naked and dislikes beauty contrived by art (Propertius)

nugae — trifles; minutiae

nugae canorae — melodius trifles (Horace)

nugis addere pondus — to add weight to trifles (Horace)

nugis armatus — armed with trifles

nulla bona — no goods; defendant has no goods for seizure

nulla dies sine linea — not a day without a line (Pliny the Elder)

nulla fides fronti — do not place any trust in appearances

nulla fides umquam miseros elegit amicos — loyalty never chose the unfortunate for friends (Lucan)

nulla lex satis commoda omnibus est — no law is sufficiently convenient to everyone (Livy)

nulla desperandum, quam diu spirat — no one should despair as long as he breathes

nullus argento color est avaris abdito terris — silver has no shine while it is hidden by the greedy from the earth (Horace)

nulli secundus — second to none

nullius addictus iurare in verba magistri — not obligated to swear to the words of any particular master

nullius filius — no one's legal son; a bastard

nullo contradicente — with nobody contradicting; without opposition

nullo dissentiente — with nobody dissenting; unanimous agreement

nullum magnum ingenium sine mixtura dementiae fuit — no great genius has every existed without a touch of madness (Seneca)

nullum quod tetigit non ornavit — he touched nothing he did not adorn

nullum scelum rationem habet — no crime is rational (Livy)

nullumiam dictum quod non sit dictun prius — nothing is ever said that has not been said before (Terence)

numerus clausus — a closed number; a prescribed quota

numini et patriae asto — I support my God and my country

numquam est fidelis cum potente societas — alliance with the powerful is never safe

nunc — now

nunc aut nunquam — now or never

Nunc Dimittis — Lord, let thy servant depart in peace (Simeon's canticle)

nunc dimittis — permission to leave; a departure

nunc est bibendum — now it's time to drink (Horace)

nunc est bibendum, nunc pede libera pulsanda tellus — now we must drink and pound the earth with each free step (Horace)

nunc pro tunc — now for then; permits retrospective action

nunc scio quid sit Amor

Now I know well what love is (Virgil)

nunc scripsi totum pro Christo da mihi potum

now that I have written so much for Christ give me a drink (from medieval manuscripts)

numquam dormio

I never sleep

numquam minus solus quam cum solus

never less alone than when alone (Cicero)

numquam non paratus

never unprepared; always prepared

nusquam tuta fides

fidelity is assured nowhere (Virgil)

O

obiit	he or she died
obiit sine prole (O.S.P.)	died without children
obiter	by the way; in passing
obiter dictum	incidental or passing remark (pl. **obiter dicta**)
obiter scriptum	incidental writing or composition (pl. **obiter scripta**)
obscuris vera involvens	covering truth with darkness (Virgil)
obscurum per obscurius	explanation which makes things more obscure
observandum	a thing to be observed
obsta principiis	resist the beginnings; stop it now (Ovid)
obstupui, steteruntque comae, et vox faucibus haesit	I was stupefied, and my hair stood on end and my voice stuck in my throat (Virgil)
occasio furem facit	opportunity makes a thief
occasionem cognosce	recognize opportunity
occupat extremum scabies	the plague takes the extreme (Horace)
occurrent nubes	clouds will intervene
O curae hominum! O quantum est in rebus inane!	O, human cares! O, how much futility is in the world!
O dea certe	O thou, who surely art a goddess (Virgil)

oderint dum metuant	let them hate me, as long as they fear me (Emperor Tiberius)
oderut di homines iniuros	the gods hate unjust men
odi et amo	I love and I hate (Catullus)
odi profanum vulgus et arceo	I hate the profane crowd, keep them away
odium	hatred; rivalry
odium aestheticum	rivalry among artists, musicians and writers
odium medicum	rivalry among those in the medical profession
odium musicum	rivalry among musicians; musical controversy
odium scholasticum	rivalry among academics about minor points
odium theologicum	rivalry among theologians about differences
odor lucri	the smell of money
O fama ingens, ingentior armis	great by fame, greater in arms
O fortunatos nimium, sua bona norint	they would be happy too if only they knew their blessings (Horace)
O imitatores, servum pecus	the servile herd of imitators (Horace)
O laborum dulce lenimen	sweet solace of labors
oleo tranquillior	smoother than oil
olet lucernam	it smells of the lamp; labored writing
oleum addere camino	to pour fuel on the stove; to make it worse

oleum perdidisti	you have lost oil (critical attack on a book)
olim meminisse iuvabit	it will be pleasant to look back on the past
omen faustum	an auspicious sign
O mihi praeteritos referat si Iuppiter annos	O that Jupiter would give me back the years that are past (Virgil)
omne aevum curae, cunctis sua displicet aetas	every age has its troubles, everyone dislikes his own age
omne bonum desuper	all good is from above
omne ignotum pro magnifico est	everything unknown seems greater than reality
omnem movere lapidem	to move every stone
omne quod dulce est cito satiat	all sweet things quickly bring satiety
omne scibile	everything knowable
omnes deteriores summa licentia	too much freedom harms everyone (Terence)
omne solum forti patria est	every soil is fatherland to a brave man (Ovid)
omne trinum est perfectum	everything in threes is perfect
omne tulit punctum qui miscuit utile dulci	he has made every point who has combined the useful and the agreeable (Horace)
omne vivum ex vivo	every living thing from a living thing
omnia ad Dei gloriam	all things for the glory of God
omnia bona bonis	to the good all things are good
omnia de super	all things are from above

omnia fert aetas, animum quoque	time bears away everything, even memory (Virgil)
omnia mala exempla ex rebus bonis orta sunt	every bad precedent originated as a justifiable measure (Sallust)
omnia mea mecum porto	I carry all my things with me
omnia mors aequat	death makes all things equal (Claudian)
omnia munda mundis	to the pure all things are pure
omnia mutantur, nihil interit	all things change, nothing dies (Ovid)
omnia mutantur, et nos mutamur in illis	all things change and we change with them
omnia praeclara rara	all excellent things are rare (Cicero)
omnia suspendens naso	turning up his nose at everything
omnia tempus alit, tempus rapit, usus in arto est	time feeds all things, time devours them, enjoyment lasts but a brief moment
omnia tuta timens	fearing all things, even safe things (Virgil)
omnia vanitas	all is vanity (Ecclesiastes)
omnia vincit amor, nos et cedamus amori	love conquers all things, let us yield to it (Virgil)
omnia vincit labor	work conquers all things (Horace)
omnia vincit veritas	truth conquers all things (Horace)
omni bihoris	every two hours

omnibus ad quos praesentes litterae pervenerint, salutem	to all to whom the present letters shall come, greetings
omnibus hoc vitium est	all have this vice (Horace)
omnibus idem	the same to all men
omnibus invideas nemo tibi	you may envy everyone but no one envied you
omnibus in rebus voluptatibus maximis fastidium finitimum est	pleasures are narrowly separated from disgust (Cicero)
omni hora	every hour
omni nocte	every night
omni quadrantae horae	every fifteen minutes
omni mane vel nocte	every morning or night
omnis amans amens	every lover is demented
omnium rerum principia parva sunt	the beginnings of all things are small (Cicero)
onus probandi	the burden of proving
onus segni impone asello	place the burden on the lazy ass
ope et consilio	with help and counsel
operae pretium est	there is reward for work (Terence)
opera illius mea sunt	his works are mine
opera omnia	complete works of an author
opere citato (op. cit.)	occurring in the work cited
opere in medio	in the middle of work
operose nihil agunt	they are busy about nothing (Seneca)
opposuit natura	nature has opposed
opprobrium medicorum	the disgrace of the doctors

optat supremo collocare Sisyphus in monte saxum
Sisyphus tries to place the boulder on top of the mountain

optima est legum interpres consuetudo
the best interpreter of the laws is custom

optima mors Parca quae venit apta die
the best death is that which comes on the day chosen by Fate (Propertius)

optimates
the aristocracy; the best people

optime
very good; excellent

optimi consiliari mortui
the best counselors are dead

optimum obsonium labor
work is the best means of eating

opum furiata cupido
the maddened lust for wealth

opus
work; composition (pl. **opera**)

opus alexandrinum
a geometrical mosaic pavement

opus artificem probat
the work proves the craftsman

opus Dei
the work of God

opus incertum
unsquared or rubble masonry

opus isodomum
masonry courses of equal height

opus manificium
manual labor, craft labor

opus magnum
a great work; a masterpiece

opus operatum
the work having been completed

opus reticulatum
reticulated or checkerboard masonry

opus spicatum	masonry in a herringbone pattern
O quam cito transit gloria mundi	how quickly passes the glory of the world (Thomas à Kempis)
ora et labora	pray and work
orare et sperare	to pray and to hope
orando laborando	by prayer and by work
ora pro nobis	pray for us
orare est laborare	to pray is to work
orate fratres	pray brothers
orate pro anima	pray for the soul
oratio gravis	a serious speech
orationem concludere	to conclude a speech
oratio obliqua	second-hand reports; hearsay
orator fit, poeta nascitur	an orator is made, a poet is born
Orbis Factor	Maker of the world
Orbis Pictus	The World in Pictures (Comenius)
orbis scientiarum	the sphere of the sciences
orbis terrarum	the earth
ordinandi lex	law of procedure
ordinatum est	it is ordered
ordines majores	superior orders: priest, deacon, subdeacon
ordines minores	minor orders: chanters, psalmists, acolytes
ordo albus	white order; Augustine order
ordo griseus	gray order; Cistercian order
ordo niger	black order; Benedictine order

ore rotundo	with a round mouth; eloquently
ore tenus	by word of mouth
origo mali	the origin of evil
O rus, quando ego te aspiciam	O country, when shall I behold thee (Horace)
O Salutaris Hostia	O saving victim (hymn of benediction of the Blessed Sacrament)
O sancta simplicitas	O holy simplicity
osculum pacis	the kiss of peace
O si sic omnes	if only everyone were like this
O tempora, O mores	O the times, O the manners (Cicero)
O terque quaterque beati	they are three or four times blessed (Virgil)
otia dant vitia	leisure engenders vices
otiosa sedulitas	laborious trifling
otium	leisure; ease
otium cum dignitate	leisure with dignity
otium sine dignitate	leisure without dignity
otium sine litteris mors est	leisure without literature is death
otium sine litteris mors est et hominis vivi sepultura	leisure without study is death, it is a tomb for the living man (Seneca)
O ubi campi?	O where are those plains? (Virgil)

P

pabulum Acheruntis food for Acheron (Plautus)

pabulum animi food for the mind

pace by grace of; in deference to

pacere occepi gravitior postquam emortuast I began to love her even more, once she died

pace tantis viris by grace of so many men

pace tua with your permission

pacta conventa the conditions agreed upon

pacta sunt servanda pacts are to be observed

pactum an agreement or legal contract

pactum nudum an informal contract; a mere promise

pactum illicitum an unlawful agreement

pactum vestitum an enforceable agreement

Paete, non dolet Paetus, it does not hurt (Arria to Paetus, husband and wife forced to commit suicide)

pallida Mors pale Death (one of the four horsemen of the Apocalypse)

palmam qui meruit ferat	let him bear the palm who has deserved it (motto of Lord Nelson and the Royal Navy)
palma non sine pulver	no palm without dust (Horace)
panem et circenses	bread and circus games (Juvenal)
Pange, lingua	sing, my tongue (a liturgical hymn)
paratae lacrimae insidias non fletum indicant	easy tears are a sign of treachery, not of true grief
parce, parce, precor	spare me, spare me, I pray
parcere subiectis, et debellare superbos	to spare those subjected and to subdue those who are proud (Virgil)
parem non fert	he endures no equal
parendo vinces	you will conquer by obedience
parens patriae	parent of his country; the sovereign
pares curiae	equals of the court
pares regni	peers of the realm
pari causa	with equal cause
pares cum paribus facillime congregantur	similar persons mingle easily with one another
pari delicto	in equal fault
pari passu	with equal pace; side by side
pari ratione	for the same reason; equally valid reason
paritur pax bello	peace is produced by war
par negotiis, neque supra	equal to his business and not above it

par nobile fratrum	a noble pair of brothers (Horace)
par oneri	equal to the burden
par pari refero	I return like for like
pars adversa	the opposing party
pars pro toto	part for the whole
partes aequales	equal parts
parti affectae applicetur	let it be applied to the affected region
particeps criminis	a partner in the crime
partitis vicibus	in individual doses
parturient montes, nascetur ridiculus mus	mountains will be in labor, and an absurd mouse will be born (Horace)
parva componere magnis	to compare small things with great
parva leves capiunt animos	small things occupy small minds (Ovid)
passim	here and there; in various places in the text
passus	a portion or a division of a poem
pateat universis per praesentes	know all men by these presents
paterfamilias	the male head of the family
Pater Filio	Father to Son (Robert Bridges)
Pater Noster	Our Father (the Lord's Prayer)
pater patriae	father of his country (Emperor Augustus)
pati necesse est multa mortalibus mala	mortal men must bear many ills

patres conscripti	fathers of the conscript; the Roman senate
patria cara, carior libertas	my country is dear, but liberty is dearer
patria est ubicumque est bene	our country is wherever we are content
patriae infelici fidelis	faithful to my unhappy country
patria potesta	parental authority
patriis virtutibus	by ancestral virtues
patris est filius	he is his father's son
pauca sed bona	few things, but good things
paucis verbis	in a few words
paulo maiora canamus	let us sing of greater things (Virgil)
paula post futurum	a little past the future
paupertas omnium artium repertix	poverty is the inventor of all arts
pax	peace
pax Britannica	British peace
pax Dei	peace of God
pax Ecclesiae	peace of the Church
pax in bello	peace in war
pax orbis terrarum	peace of the world
pax paritur bello	peace is produced by war
pax potior bello	peace is more powerful than war
paz quaeritur bello	peace is sought by war
pax regis	the king's peace
pax Romana	Roman peace; area subject to Roman law
pax tecum	peace be with you (singular)

pax vobiscum	peace be with you (plural)
peccare pauci nolunt, nulli nesciunt	few are unwilling to do wrong, all know how
peccavi	I have sinned; I was wrong
pectus est quod disertos facit	the heart makes men eloquent (Quintilian)
pecuniae cause	for the sake of wealth
pecuniae obodiunt omnia	all things yield to money
pecunia non olet	money does not smell
pecunia regimem est rerum omniun	money rules over all things
pedes muscarum	feet of flies; system of musical notation
peior est bello timor ipse belli	worse than war is the very fear of war
Pelio imponere Ossam	to pile Mount Ossa on Mount Pelion
Pelio imposuisse Olympo	to have piled Pelion on Olympus (Horace)
pelle moras, brevis est magni Fortuna favoris	make haste, the flood tide of Fortune soon ebbs
penates	household gods of the Romans
pendente lite	the lawsuit is pending
pentralia mentis	the innermost thoughts of a person
per accidens	by accident; by chance
per acria belli	through the bitterness of war
per ambages	by circuitous ways; indirect manner
per angusta ad augusta	through anguish to honors

per annum	per year, annually
per ardua ad astra	through adversity to the stars (motto of the Royal Air Force)
per aspera ad astra	through difficulties to the stars
per capita	by head (of population); for each person
per centum	by the hundred; in every hundred
per contra	on the other hand; a contrary position
per curiam	by the whole court
per diem	by the day, each day
pereant qui ante nos nostra dixerunt	may they perish who have expressed their bright ideas before us
pereunt et imputantur	(the hours) pass away and are reckoned
per essentiam	by essential means
per eundem	by the same
per extensum	at length
per fas et nefas	through right and wrong
perfidia Punica	Punic treachery
perfidium ingenium	extreme enthusiasm or ardor
per gradus	step by step
periculum fortitudine evasi	by courage I have escaped danger
periculum in mora	danger in delay
perierat totus orbis, nisi iram finiret misericordia	the whole world would perish if pity did not assuage anger (Seneca)
per impossibile	as is impossible
per incuriam	through carelessness

per infortunium	by accident, fortuitous
per interim	meanwhile
periuria ridet amantum Iuppiter	Jupiter laughs at lovers' lies (Tibullus)
per jocum	in jest, as a joke
per Jovem	by Jove, by Jupiter
per mare per terram	by land and by sea
per mense	by the month
per mensem	by months; for each month
per mille	by the thousand
per minas	by threats
permitte divis cetera	leave the rest to the gods (Horace)
per os	by mouth
per pares	by one's peers
perpetuum mobile	perpetual motion
per procurationem	by action of an agent
per quod	through which; by which
per recto et retro	forward and backward
per saltum	by a single leap
per se	by itself; inherently
per se esse	to be by itself
per se subsistere perseverando	to subsist by persevering
persona	person, character or role
persona ficta	a fictitious person
persona grata	an acceptable person; a welcome person
persona gratissima	a most acceptable person
persona muta	a silent actor
persona non grata	an unacceptable person; an unwelcome person

persta atque obdura	be steadfast and endure
per stirpes	through the roots or stock; by representation
per totam curiam	by the entire court
per various casus, per tot discrimina rerum	through many mishaps, and through the many trials of fortune (Virgil)
per veritatem vis	through truth, power (motto of Washington University)
per viam	by the way of
per viam dolorosam	by the sorrowful path
per vias rectas	by straight roads
per vivam vocem	by the living voice
pessimi exempli	of a very bad example
pessimum genus inimicorum laudantes	flatterers are the worst sort of enemies
pessimum inimicorum genus, laudantes	the worst class of men, those who praise
petitio principii	begging the question, a logical fallacy
phiala prius agitata	the bottle first being shaken
philosophia mundi	a philosophy of the world
Pia Desideria	things religiously desired (manifesto of the Pietistic movement)
pia fraus	pious fraud
pietas	honor and respect for one's ancestors
pinxit	he or she painted it
placebo	I shall please

Placebo Domino in regione vivorum
I shall be acceptable to the Lord (Psalm 116) (hymn sung in the vespers for the dead)

placet
it pleases; to give an assenting vote

placidaque ibi demum morte quievit
and there he reposed in tranquil death (Virgil)

placitum
decree, decision

plaudite, cives
applaud, citizens

pleno jure
with full right

plenum dominium
full ownership

ploratur lacrimis amissa pecunia veris
one sheds real tears when one loses one's own money (Juvenal)

plures crapula quam gladius
drinking (kills) more (people) than the sword

plus dolet quam necesse est, qui ante dolet quam necesse sit
he suffers more than is necessary, who suffers before it is necessary (Seneca)

plus salis, quam sumptus
more of good taste than expense (Nepos)

plus vident oculi quam oculus
eyes see more than an eye; two heads are better than one

poena corporalis
through corporal punishment

poesis est vinum daemonum
poetry is the devil's wine

poeta nascitur, non fit
a poet is born, not made

pollice compresso
thumbs folded; sign of approval

pollice verso
thumbs down; sign of disapproval

pons asinorum	the ass's bridge; any problem which is too difficult for neophytes to solve (Euclid)
pontifex maximus	the head of priests in ancient Rome; the pope
pontificalia	the vestments and insignia of a clergyman
populus me sibilat, at mihi plaudo	the people hiss at me, but I applaud myself (Horace)
populus vult decipi, ergo decipiatur	the people want to be deceived, therefore let them be deceived
porro unum est necessarium	still there is one thing necessary
posse comitatus	group of men able to serve as deputies
posse videor	I seem to be able
possunt, quia posse videntur	they can because they seem to be able (Virgil)
post bellum auxilium	help after the war
post cibum	after meals
post cineres gloria sera venit	after one is reduced to ashes, fame comes too late (Martial)
post diem	after the day
post equitem sedet atra cura	behind the horseman sits black care (Horace)
post factum nullum consilium	after the act, no advice is useful
post festum venisti	you have arrived after the feast

post hoc, ergo propter hoc	after this, therefore because of this; fallacy that temporal succession implies causality
post litem motam	after litigation began
post meridiem (P.M.)	after noon
post mortem	after death; an autopsy
post natum	born after
post nubila Phoebus	after the clouds, Phoebus
post obitum	after death
post partum	after childbirth
post proelia praemia	after battles come the rewards
post res	after things
post scriptum (P.S.)	an addition to a letter after the signature
post tenebras lux	after darkness, light
post terminum	after the conclusion
post tot naufragia portum	after so many shipwrecks, the port
postulata	fundamental assumptions
potior est qui prior est	the one who is earlier is preferred
potius mori quam foedari	rather to die than to be dishonored
praecognitum	something known beforehand
praecipe	a written order or command
praedia bellica	goods confiscated in war
praedium	land, property, estate
praefervidum ingenium Scotorum	the ardently serious manner of the Scots

praemissas sentias
aforesaid statements; premises

praemonitus, praemunitus
forewarned, forearmed

praemunire
statutes for the punishment of advocates of papal jurisdiction in England in 1529

praestat cautela quam medela
prevention is better than the cure

praestat sero quam nunquam
better late than never

praestatur laus virtuti, sed multo ocius verno gelu tabescit
praise is bestowed on virtue but vanished more quickly than frost in the spring

praesto et persto
I stand in front and I stand firm

praesumitur pro negante
it is presumed for the negative

praeteriti anni
the bygone years

precibus infirmis
with abject prayers (Livy)

pretium
value; worth; price

pretium affectionis
the price of affection

pretium laborum non vile
no vile reward for the labors

pretium periculi
premium for insurance

pretium puellae
the price of the maiden

prima facie
on the face; on first sight

primaria ecclesia
the mother church

primo
in first place

primogenitus
the first-born son

primo intuiti
at first glance

primum cognitum
the first thing known

primum mobile — the first source of motion or action

primum non nocere — first of all, do not harm

primus inter pares — first or foremost among equals

primus urbes inter, divum domus, aurea Roma — first among cities, home of the gods, golden Rome

principia, non homines — principles, not men

principibus plaucisse viri non ulima laus est — to have won the approval of men is not the lowest praise (Horace)

principiis obsta — resist the beginnings (Ovid)

principiorum non est ratio — there is no reasoning of principles

principium individuationis — principle of individuation

prior pententi — to the person applying first

prior tempore, prior iure — first in time, first in right

pristinae virtutis memores — remembering the valor of former days

privatum commodum publico cedit — private goods yield to the public

privilegium clericale — benefit of the clergy

pro aris et focis — for altars and hearths

probatum est — it has been proved

probis probatum potius quam multis fore — the praise of honorable men is worth more than that of a multitude

probitas laudatur et alget — honesty is praised and is neglected (Juvenal)

probitas bono publico — honesty (promotes) the public good

pro bono et malo	for good and bad
pro bono publico	for the public good
probum non poenitet	the honest man does not repent
procendendo	duty to have a court proceed to judgment
procul este, profani	be gone, you who are profane (Virgil)
pro Deo et Ecclesia	for God and the Church
pro Deo et patria	for God and country (motto of the American University)
prodesse quam conspici	to be useful rather than to be admired
pro et contra	(reasons) for and against an argument
profanum vulgus	the profane multitude; the common people
pro forma	as a formality; for the sake of form
pro hac vice	for this turn; for this specific occasion
proletarius	person of poor economic condition
pro libertate patriae	for the liberty of my country
pro memoria	for a memorial
promotor fidei	promoter of the faith
pro mundi beneficio	for the benefit of the world
pro nunc	for now
pro patria	for the country
pro patria, pro liberis, pro aris atque focis suis certare	to struggle for our country, our children, our altars, and our hearths (Sallust)

propositi tenax	firm of purpose
propria quae maribus	things appropriate to husbands
proprie communia dicere	to speak commonplace ideas as if original
proprietates verborum	proper meanings of words
proprio jure	of one's own right
proprio motu	by one's own motion or initiative
proprio vigore	of one's own strength
proprium humani ingenii est odisse quem laeseris	it is human nature to hate a person whom you have harmed (Tacitus)
propter	on account of
propter hoc	on this account
pro pudore	for shame
pro rata	in proportion, as a given ratio
pro rata parte	according to a calculated part
pro ratione aetatis	according to a patient's age
pro rege, lege, et grege	for the king, the law, and the people
pro re nata	for any occasion; as needed
pro salute animi	for the welfare of the soul
pro scientia et religione	for science and religion (motto of Denver University)
pro se	for one's self; in one's own behalf
prosequitur	he prosecutes; he pursues the case

prosit	may it benefit you; to your fortune
pro tanto	to such an extent; for so much
protectio trahit subjectionem	protection draws with it subjection
pro tempore	temporarily, for the moment
pro virili parte	for a man's part
provisione quod	it being provided that
proxime accessit	he came nearest; the runner-up
proximo mense	in the next month
proximum genus	nearest kind
proximus ardet Ucalegon	Ucalegon's house next door is burning
prudens futuri	considering the future
purdens quaestio dimidium scientiae	half of the knowledge is being able to ask the right question (Francis Bacon)
publice	in a public manner
publici juris	of the public right
pudor doceri non potest innatus potest	modesty must be innate, it cannot be learned
pugnis et calcibus	with fists and heels
pulvis et umbra sumus	we are but dust and shadows (Horace)
punctatim	point for point
punctum	point or dot
punctum caecum	a blind spot
punctum contra punctum	note against note; counterpoint
punctum saliens	a salient point
punctum temporis	point of time
punctum vegetationis	a growing point

Q

qua	in the capacity of
quacumque via data	which way you take it
Qua Cursum Ventus	Where the Winds (guide) their Course (Clough)
quadragesima	fortieth; forty days before Easter
quadrivium	arithmetic, geometry, astronomy, and music
quae amissa salva	lost things are safe
quaecumque sunt vera	whatsoever things are true (motto of Northwestern University)
quaedam iura non scripta, sed omnibus scriptis certiora sunt	some written laws are more firmly established than all written laws
quae est eadem	which is the same
quae fuerunt vitia mores sunt	what once were vices are now customs
quae nocent docent	things that hurt, teach
quae pars orationis?	what part of speech?
quaere	question; inquire
quaerenda pecunia primum est, virtus post nummos	money is the first thing to be sought, good reputation after wealth (Horace)
quaere verum	seek the truth
quaeritur	it is sought; a question arises

quaesitum	that which is sought after; a solution
quaestio vexata	a much debated question
quae sursum volo videre	I desire to see things that are above
quae vide	which (things) see
quais dicat	as if one should say
qualis	of what kind
qualis ab incepto	such from the beginning (Horace)
qualis artifex pereo	what an artist dies in me (Nero)
qualis pater talis filius	like father like son
qualis rex, talis grex	like king, like people
qualis vita, finis ita	as in life, so is the end
quam diu se bene gesserit	as long as he conducts himself well
quam parva sapietnia mundus regitur	with how little wisdom the world is governed
quam primum	as soon as possible
quam proxime	as nearly as possible
quam te Deus esse iussit	what God commanded you to be
quandoque bonus dormitat Homerus	sometimes even good Homer sleeps
quanti est sapere	what a great thing to be wise (Terence)
quantum	as much as; how much
quantum libet	as much as one pleases
quantum meruit	as much as was deserved
quantum mutatus ab illo	how changed from what he once was
quantum placeat	as much as pleases
quantum satis	as much as is sufficient

quantum sufficit	as much as necessary
quantum valeat	as much as it may be worth
quantum vis	as much as you wish
quaque hora	at every hour
quare clausum fregit	wherefore he broke the close; trespass
quare impedit	why does he obstruct? why is he fighting us?
quarterni terminorum	logical fallacy of four terms
quarto die post	on the fourth day after
quasi dicutum	as if said
quater in die	four times a day
quem di diligunt adulescens moritur, dum valet sentit sapit	he whom the gods love dies young while he has his strength and senses
quem quaeritis?	whom do you seek?
quem res plus nimio delectavere secundae mutatae quatient	those whom prosperity has charmed too much, adveristy will shatter (Horace)
qui bene amat bene castigat	he who loves well chastises well
qui bene distinguit bene docet	he who makes good distinctions teaches well
qui desiderat pacem praeparet bellum	let him who wants peace prepare for war (Vegetius)
qui docet discit	he who teaches learns
qui facit per alium facit per se	he who does a thing through another does it through himself
qui fugiebat rursus proeliabitur	he who has fled will do battle once more

qui interrogat bene docet	he who questions (well) teaches well
qui invidet minor est	he who envies is inferior
qui ipse si sapiens prodesse nequit, nequiquam sapit	a wise man whose wisdom does not serve him is wise in vain
qui laborat orat	he who works prays
qui male agit odit lucem	he who acts badly hates the light
qui me amat, amat et canem meam	he who loves me loves my dog
qui nescit dissimulare nescit vivere	he who does not know how to dissemble does not know how to live
qui nimium multis "non amo" dicit, amat	he who often says "I love not" is in love (Ovid)
qui nimium probat nihil probat	he who proves too much, proves nothing
qui non negat fatetur	he who does not deny, admits
qui non proficit deficit	he who does not make progress fails
qui non vetat peccare, cum possit, iubet	he who does not forbid sin, commands it
qui parcit nocentibus innocentes punit	he who spares the guilty punishes the innocent
qui scribit bis legit	he who writes reads twice
qui stat, caveat ne cadat	let him who stands beware lest he fall
qui tacet, consentire videntur	he who remains silent seems to consent
qui tacet consentit	he who remains silent consents
qui tam	who as well
qui timide rogat docet negare	he who asks timidly invites refusal

qui transtulit sustinet	He who transplanted sustains (motto of Connecticut)
qui uti scit ei bona	he who knows how to use wealth should have it (Terence)
qui vicit non est victor nisi victus fatetur	the winner is not truly the winner unless the loser admits it
qui vive?	who goes there? a sentry's challenge
quia timet	because he fears
quicquid delirant reges, plectuntur Achivi	whatever blunder the kings commit, the Greeks themselves suffer
quicquid multis peccatur, inultum est	crimes perpetuated by the multitude remain unavenged (Lucan)
quicunque vult servari	whosoever wants to be saved (Athanasian Creed)
quid est veritas?	what is truth? (Gospel of John)
quid faciendum	what's to be done?
quid hoc sibi vult?	what does this mean?
quid leges sine moribus vanae proficiunt?	what can laws accomplish in the absence of morals? (Horace)
quid novi?	what's new?
quid nunc?	what now?
quid pro quo	something for something
quid rides? mutato nomine de te fabula narratur	why do you laugh? change the name and the story is yours (Horace)

quid sit futurum cras, fuge quaerere	avoid asking what tomorrow will bring (Horace)
quid times?	what do you fear?
quid verum atque decens	what is true and becoming
quidam	someone; an unknown person
quidditas	whatness; essence of a substance
quidquid agis prudenter agas	whatever you do, do with caution
quieta non movere	do not move quiet things
quis custodiet ipsios custodes?	who is to control the authorities? (Juvenal)
quis fallere possit amantem?	who can deceive a lover? (Virgil)
quis separabit	who shall separate us? (Order of St. Patrick)
quis vitia odit, homines odit	he who hates vice, hates mankind
quisque sibi proximus	everyone is nearest to himself
quo animo?	with what intention?
quo Fata vocant	where the Fates call
quo jure?	by what right? on what authority?
quo mihi fortunam, si non condeditur uti?	what is fortune to me if I cannot enjoy it? (Horace)
quo pax gloria ducunt	where peace and glory lead
quo usque	how long; how far
quo usque tandem abutere patientia nostra?	how long will you abuse our patience? (Cicero)

quo vadis?	where are you going?
quo warranto?	by what right or authority?
quoad	as regards; so far as
quoad hoc	as to this; in this respect
quoad minus	as to the lesser matter
quoad ultra	as regards the past
quocunque modo	in whatsoever manner
quocunque nomine	under whatsoever name
quod absurdum est	which thing is absurd
quod ad hoc	as far as this; to this extent
quod avertat Deus	which may God avert
quod bene notandum	which is to be well noted
quod cibus est aliis, aliis est venenum	what is food to some is poison to others
quod cito acquiritur cito perit	that which is quickly gained is quickly lost
quod erat demonstrandum (Q.E.D)	that which was to be proved
quod erat faciendum (Q.E.F.)	that which was to be done
quod erat inveniendum	that which was to be found
quod est	which is
quod hoc sibi vult?	what does this mean?
quod necessitas cogit, defendit	that which necessity compels, it justifies
quod nimis miseri volunt, hoc facile credunt	what the wretched desire to excess, they often easily believe
quod non opus est, asse carum est	what is not necessary is dear as a penny
quod quo est	that by which it is

quod nota	which note; which mark
quod sciam	as far as I know (Cicero)
quod scripsi scripsi	what I have written I have written
quod semper, quod ubique, quod ab omnibus	what (has been held) always, everywhere and by everyone
quod vide (q.v.)	for which to see; refer to
quodlibet	subtle point in an argument
quomodo?	in what manner?
quomodo vales?	how are you?
quondam	former, once
quorum pars magna fui	in which I played a great part
quos deus vult perdere prius dementat	whom a god wishes to destroy, he first makes mad (adapted from Euripides)
quot homines, tot sententiae	so many men, so many opinions (Terence)
quot servi, tot hostes	so many servants, so many enemies
quotidie	daily
quoties	whenever
quovis modo	in whatever manner

R

radit usque ad cutem — he shaves all the way to the skin

radix malorum — the root of all evil (reference to avarice)

radix omnium malorum est cupiditas — the desire for money is the root of all evil

rara avis — a rare bird; an unusual person

rara avis in terris nigroque simillima cygno — a rare bird upon the earth and very much like a black swan

raram facit mixturam cum sapientia forma — beauty and brains are seldom found together (Petronius)

rari nantes — a few swimming here and there (Virgil)

rata — rate; individual share of a whole

ratio decidendi — the essentials of a judgment

ratio est radius divini luminis — reason is a ray of divine light

ratio legis — the underlying principle or reasoning

ratione juris — by principle of one's right

ratione materiae — by reason of the subject matter

ratione soli — by reason of the soil

rebus sic stantibus	things being the way they are
re	in the matter of; concerning
recta ratio	right reason
recte et suaviter	justly and mildly
recto	the right-hand page of a book
rectus in curia	upright in court
reddendo singula singulis	by referring each to each
reddite quae sunt Caesaris Caesari, et quae sunt Dei Deo	render unto Caesar things that are Caesar's and unto God the things that are God's (Synoptic Gospels)
redime te captum quam queas minimo	when taken prisoner, pay as little as you can to buy your freedom
redintegratio amoris	the renewal of love
redire ad nuces	to return to the nuts
redivivus	brought back to life
redolet lucernam	it smells of the lamp; labored writing
reductio ad absurdum	pursuing a proposition to absurd limits
reductio ad impossibile	reduction to the impossible
reductus in pulverem	reduced to powder
regia via	the royal way; king's highway
Regina Caeli	Queen of Heaven; the Virgin Mary
regina Dei gratia	queen by the grace of God
regium donum	a royal gift

Regius Professor	Royal Professor; title in English schools
regnat populus	the people rule (motto of Arkansas)
regula fidei	rule of faith
re infecta	the thing being unfinished
rei publicae	in matters of the state
relata refero	I tell it as it was told to me
religio laici	a layman's religion
religio loci	the religion of the place
religio medici	religion of the physician
reliquiae	the remains
rem acu tetigisti	you've touched the thing with a needle
remisso animo	with a relaxed mind
remis velisque	with oars and sails; a total effort
remittitur	diminishing a verdict of a jury by subtraction
rem tene, verba sequentur	grasp the matter, the words will follow
renovate animos	renew your courage
renovato nomine	by a revived name
repente dives nemo factus est bonus	no one who is rich is made suddenly good (Publius Syrus)
re perfecta	the thing being finished
repertorium	a catalog
repetatur	let it be repeated
requies, aeterna	eternal rest
requiem aeternam dona eis, Domine	grant them eternal rest, O Lord (Requiem Mass)

requiescat in pace (R.I.P.)	may he or she rest in peace
requiescit in pace	he or she rests in peace
rerum concordia discors	the harmony of nature in discord (Horace)
rerum primordia	the beginnings of things
res	the thing; the subject matter of an action
res accedent luminis rebus	one light shines upon others
res age, tute eris	stay busy and you will be safe
res adjudicata	the decision of the court
res alienae	things belonging to others
res angusta domi	strained situations at home; difficult times
res cogitans	thinking substance; the mind (Descartes)
res controversa	things in controversy
res corporales	tangible things
res derelicta	abandoned property
res est ingeniosa dare	giving requires good sense (Ovid)
res est sacra miser	a person in distress is a sacred thing
res est solliciti plena timoris amor	love is full of anxious fears (Ovid)
res extensa	extended substance (Descartes)
res extra mentem	things outside the mind
res gestae	material facts: matters relevant to a lawsuit
res in cardine est	the matter is on a door hinge; a turning point
res incorporales	intangible things

res inter alios	a matter between other people
res ipsa loquitur	the thing speaks for itself; obvious situation
res judicata	thing which has been judged; a settled matter
res judicata pro veritate	a decided case is considered as a law
res mobiles	movable things
res nihili	thing of no consequence; a trifling matter
res non posse creari de nilo	matter cannot be created from nothing (Lucretius)
res nullius	things belonging to nobody; abandoned property
respice, adspice, prospice	examine the past, examine the present, examine the future (motto of the City College of New York)
respice finem	examine the end; look to the end
respondeat superior	let the superior reply and be responsible
res publica	the affairs of the people; Roman commonwealth
res rustica	a country matter
resurgam	I shall rise again
retro Satana	get thee behind me, Satan
re vera	in truth; in fact
revocate animos	recover your courage
rex bibendi	king of drinking
rex Dei gratia	king by the grace of God
Rex Iudaeorum	King of the Jews

rex non potest peccare	the king can do no wrong
rex nunquam moritur	the king never dies
rex regnat sed non gubernat	the king reigns but does not govern
rex regum	the king of kings
ridentem dicere verum quid vetat?	what hinders one from speaking the truth even while laughing? (Horace)
ridere in stomacho	to laugh inside one's self
ride si sapis	laugh if you are wise (Martial)
ridiculus mus	a ridiculous mouse (Horace)
rigor mortis	stiffness of a corpse occurring after death
risum teneatis, amici?	could you help laughing, my friends? (Horace)
risus	laughter
rituale	a manual for priests
rixatur de lana saepe caprina	he often quarrels about goat's wool (Horace)
Roma peditae	pilgrims who travel to Rome on foot
ruat caelum	though the heavens fall
rudis indigestaque moles	a rude and undigested mass (Ovid)
rus in urbe	countryside in the city (Martial)

S

Sacrum Romanum Imperium	the Holy Roman Empire
saepe stilum vertas	often turn the stylus (Horace)
saepe ignavavit fortem ex spe expectatio	expectation based on hope often deludes courageous men
saeva indignatio	fierce wrath (Virgil)
saevis tranquillus in undis	calm in the midst of waves
sal	salt
sal amarum	bitter salt
sal Atticum	Attic salt; intellectual wit
sal catharticus	Epsom salt
sal culinarius	common salt
sal gemmae	rock salt
sal sapit omnia	salt seasons everything
salus mundi	the welfare of the world
salus per Christum Redemptorem	salvation through Christ the Redeemer
salus populi	welfare of the people
salus populi suprema lex ecto	the safety of the people is the supreme law (motto of Missouri) (adapted from Cicero)
salus rei publicae suprema lex	the welfare of the state is the supreme law

salus ubi multi consiliari	when there are many advisers, there is safety
salva conscientia	without compromising one's conscience
salva dignitate	without compromising one's dignity
salva fide	without breaking one's faith
salvam fac reginam, O Domine	God save the queen
salva res est	the matter is safe (Terence)
Salvator mundi	Savior of the world
salve	hail; welcome
Salve, Regina Misericordiae	Hail, Queen of Mercy (Catholic hymn)
salvo iure	saving the right
sal volatile	volatile salt; ammonium carbonate
salvo ordine	with regard to one's rank
salvo pudore	without violation of modesty
salvo sensu	without violation of sense
salvum fac regem, O Domine	God save the king
sanae mentis	of sound mind
sancta simplicitas	holy simplicity
sancte et sapienter	with holiness and wisdom
Sanctus	hymn which concludes preface to the Eucharist
sanctus sanctorum	holy of holies; sacred retreat; private room
sapere aude	dare to be wise (Horace)

sapiens dominabitur astris	a wise man will rule the stars
sapiens nihil affirmat quod non probat	a wise man states as true nothing he cannot prove
Sartor Resartus	the tailor retailored (Thomas Carlyle)
sat cito, si sat bene	soon enough, but well enough (Cato the Elder)
satis	enough
satis diu vel natura vixi, vel gloria	I have lived long enough, both in years and in accomplishments (Julius Caesar)
satis eloquentiae, sapientiae panum	too much eloquence, too little wisdom
satis est superare inimicum, nimium est perdere	it is enough to defeat the enemy, too much to ruin him
satis quod sufficit	what suffices is enough
satis superque	enough and some to spare
satis verborum	enough of words
sat pulchra, si sat bona	beautiful enough, if she is good enough
Saturnalia regna	the reign of Saturn; the golden age (Virgil)
scaenae frons	ornamental facade; stage background
scandalum magnatum	scandal of exalted persons
scelus intra se tacitum qui cogitat ullum crimen habet	he who silently meditates a crime is already guilty (Juvenal)
scienter	previous knowledge of the facts of a case
scientia	knowledge; science

scientia est potentia	knowledge is power
scientia gratia scientiae	knowledge for the sake of knowledge
scientia intuitiva	intuitive knowledge
scientia popinae	the science of cooking
scientia sol mentis est	knowledge is the sun of the mind (motto of the University of Delaware)
scientia scientiarum	the science of sciences
scilicet	it is permitted to know
scio cui credidi	I know in whom I have believed
scire facias	cause it to be known; allow enforcement
scire feci	I have caused to know
scire licet	it is permitted to know
scire mori sors prima viris, sed proxima cogi	man's first happiness is to know how to die, his second is to be forced to die (Lucan)
scribendi recte sapere est et principium et fons	the foundation and source of writing well is to be wise (Horace)
scribere est agere	to write is to act
scribere iussit amor	love made me write (Ovid)
scribere scientes	skilled in writing
scribimus indocti doctique	learned and unlearned, we write (Horace)
scripsi	I have written
scripsit	he or she wrote it
scriptor classicus	aristocratic writer; writer for the few
scriptor proletarius	proletarian writer; writer for the masses

sculpsit	he or she carved it
scuto bonae voluntatis tuae coronasti nos	with the shield of Thy good favor Thou hast encompassed us (Great Seal of Maryland)
secretum iter et fallentis semita vitae	a quiet journey in the untrodden path of life (Horace)
secundi adjacentis	a proposition in logic lacking a connective
secundum	according to; beside or next to
secundum aequum et bonum	according to what is just and right
secundum artem	according to art
secundum bonos mores	according to good manners
secundum formam statuti	according to the form of the statute
secundum genera	according to classes
secundum legem	according to law
secundum naturam	according to nature
secundum ordinem	according to sequence; in proper order
secundum quid	according to something; in some respect
secundum regulam	according to rule
secundum usum	according to usage
secundum veritatem	according to truth
securis iudicat orbis terrarum	the verdict of the world is conclusive
se defendendo	in self-defense
sedente animo	with a settled mind
sederunt	a formal meeting of an ecclesiastical body

sedes	the formal see of a bishop
sed fugit interea, fugit inreparabile tempus	but time moves inexorably and will never return (Virgil)
sed haec hactenus	but so much for this
seditio civium hostium est occasio	sedition of the citizens is an opportunity for the enemy
sed quaere	but inquire; examine further
segnius homines bona quam mala sentiunt	men are slower to recognize blessings than evils (Livy)
sella curulis	official seat; seat of honor
semel	once
semel abbas, semper abbas	once an abbot, always an abbot
semel et simul	once and together
semel insanivimus omnes	we have all been mad once
semel pro semper	once and for all
semi	a half
semi hora	half an hour
semitae sapientiae	paths of wisdom
semper	always
semper ad eventum festinat	he always hurries to the crisis
semper avarus eget, certum voto pete finem	one who covets is always a beggar, place a limit on your wishing (Horace)
semper eadem	always the same (motto of Queen Elizabeth)
semper ego auditor tantum?	am I always to be only a listener? (Juvenal)

semper et ubique	always and everywhere
semper felix	always fortunate
semper fidelis	always faithful (motto of U.S. Marine Corps)
semper idem	always the same thing
semper paratus	always prepared (motto of U.S. Coast Guard)
semper specialia generalibus insunt	particular things are always included in general things
semper timidum scelus	crime is always fearful
semper vivit in armis	he always lives in arms
senatus consultum	a decree of the senate
Senatus Populusque Romanus	the Roman Senate and People (S.P.Q.R.)
senex bis puer	an old man twice a boy; second childhood
senilis dementia	insanity occurring as the result of old age
seniores priores	elders first
sensibilia communia	common sensibles; qualities of an object that may be perceived by several senses
sensu bono	in a good sense
sensu malo	in a bad sense
sensu stricto	strictly speaking
sententia facit jus	judgment creates right
separatio a mensa et toro	separation from bed and board
separatio a vinculo matrimonii	separation from the bond of matrimony
septimana	one week
septuagesima	the seventieth day before Easter

Septuaginta	Greek translation of the Hebrew scripture made in 275 B.C. by seventy scholars
sepultus	buried
sequens (seq.)	the following
sequitur	it follows; the following remark
sequiturque patrem non passibus aequis	he follows his father, but not with equal steps (Virgil)
sequor non inferior	I follow (but I am) not inferior
seriatim	in due order; successive; one by one
sermo index animi	speech is an index of the mind
sero	too late
sero sapiunt Phryges	the Phrygians became wise too late
sero sed serio	late, but seriously
sero venientibus ossa	for latecomers, the bones
serus in caelum redeas	may you return late to heaven
servabo fidem	I will keep the faith
serva iugum	preserve the yoke
servare modum	keep within the bounds
servata fides cineri	faithful to the ashes (of one's ancestors)
servitutem mortalitati at malitiam viae sunt	to some extent liken slavery to death
Servus Servorum Dei	Servant of the Servants of God; the Pope
sesquipedalia verba	words that are a foot and half long

sexagesima	sixtieth day before Easter
sic	thus, so, as it was, in this way
sic donec	thus until
sic eunt fata hominum	thus go the destinies of men
sic in originali	thus in the original
sic itur ad astra	thus one goes to the stars
sic iuheo	thus I order
si contingat	if it happens
sic me servavit Apollo	thus Apollo saved me (Horace)
si componere magnis parva mihi fas est	if I may be allowed to compare small things with great things (Ovid)
sic passim	thus throughout (the text)
sic semper tyrannis	thus ever to tyrants (motto of Virginia)
sic transit gloria mundi	thus passes the glory of the world (Thomas à Kempis)
sicut meus et mos	as is my habit (Horace)
sicut patribus, sit Deus nobis	as with our fathers, may God be with us
sic volo sic iubeo	I want it this way; I order it this way
si Deus nobiscum, quis contra nos?	if God be with us, who shall be against us?
si dis placet	if it pleases the gods
si fecisti nega	if you did it, deny it
si finis bonus est, tonlm bonum erit	if the end is good, everything will be good
si foret in terris, rideret Democritus	if we were on earth, Democritus would laugh
si fortuna iuvat	if fortune favors

sigillum	a seal
signetur	let it be labeled
si latet ars, prodest	if the art is hidden, it succeeds
sile et philosophus esto	be silent and be a philosopher
silentium altum	deep silence
silent leges inter arma	laws are silent in the midst of war (Cicero)
similia similibus curantur	like things are cured by likes
similia similibus percipiuntur	like things are perceived through like things
similis simili gaudet	like takes pleasure in like
similiter	likewise
si monumentum requiris, circumspice	if you seek a monument, look around you (reference to St. Paul's Cathedral)
simplex munditiis	simple in neatness (Horace)
simpliciter	plainly, frankly
simul et semel	together and at one time
si natura negat, facit indignatio versum	when talent fails, indignation writes the verse (Juvenal)
sincerum est nisi vas, quodcumque infundis acescit	unless the vessel is clean, everything you pour into it turns sour (Horace)
sine	without
sine anno	without a year
sine Cerere et Libero friget Venus	without Ceres and Bacchus, Venus grows cold
sine cortice natare	to swim without corks

sine cruce, sine luce	without the Cross, without the light
sine cura	without care
sine die	without a day
sine dubio	without doubt
sine ictu	without a blow
sine invidia	without envy
sine ira	without anger
sine joco	without joking
sine ira est studio	without anger and bias
sine loco, anno, vel nomine	without place, date or name
sine loco et anno	without place and date
sine legitima prole	without lawful children
sine mascula prole	without male children
sine mora	without delay
sine nervis	without strength
sine nomine	without name
sine odio	without hatred
sine omni periculo	without any danger
sine praeiudicio	without prejudice
sine proba causa	without probable cause
sine prole	without children
sine qua non	without which not; a fundamental condition
singulatim	one by one; singly
singulorum	of each hand
sinistra manu	with the left hand
si opus sit	if it becomes necessary
si parva licet componere magnis	if it is allowed to compare small things with great things (Virgil)

si peccavi, insciente feci	if I have sinned, I had no intention of doing so (Terence)
si post fata venit gloria non propero	if glory comes after death, I am not in a hurry (Martial)
si quaeris peninsulam amoenam circumspice	if you seek a lovely peninsula, look about you (motto of Michigan)
si quis	if anyone
si sic omnes	if everything were thus
si sit prudentia	if there is prudence
siste viator	stop, traveler (tombstone inscription)
sit non doctissima coniux	may your wife not be very learned (Martial)
sit pro ratione voluntas	let will stand for reason (Juvenal)
sit tibi terra levis	may the earth be light upon you (on tombstones)
sit ut est, aut non sit	let it be as it is, or let it not be
sit venia verbis	let these words be pardoned
si vis amari ama	if you wish to be loved, love (Seneca)
si vis me flere dolendum est primum ipsi tibi	if you wish me to weep, you yourself must first feel grief (Horace)
si vis pacem, para bellum	if you want peace, prepare for war (Vegetius)
socius criminis	an associate in crime
sola iuvat virtus	virtue alone helps one

sola nobilitas virtus	virtue alone is true nobility
sola salus servire Deo	our only safety is in serving God
sola virtus invicta	virtue alone is invincible
solem quis dicere falsum audeat?	who would dare to call the sun a liar?
soli Deo gloria	glory to God alone
solitudinem faciunt pacem appellant	they create desolation and call it peace (Tacitus)
sol lucet omnibus	the sun shines for everyone
solus	alone
solventur risu tabulae	the indictments are dismissed with laughter (Horace)
solvitur ambulando	it is solved by walking (by practice)
solvitur acris hiems	the harsh winter is melting away (Horace)
sortes	divination by opening a book
sortes Biblicae	divination using the Bible
sortes Homericae	divination using Homer's works
sortes Virgilianae	divination using Virgil's works
spargere voces in vulgum ambiguas	to spread an equivocal rumor among the crowd (Virgil)
speciali gratia	by special favor
spectatum veniunt, veniunt spectentur ut ipsae	they come to see, they come that they may be seen (Ovid)

spectemur agendo	let us be judged by our · actions
speculum vitae	mirror of life
spem pretio non emo	I do not buy mere hope (Terence)
spem sine corpore amat, corpus putat esse, quod umbra est	he loves an unsubstantial hope and trusts in a substance which is only a shadow
sperat infestis, metuit secundis	he hopes in adversity and fears in prosperity (Horace)
speravi	I have hoped
spero meliora	I hope for better things
spes	hope
spes bona	good hope
spes gregis	the hope of the flock (Virgil)
spes mea Christus	Christ is my hope
spes mea in Deo	my hope is in God
spes sibi quisque	let each rely upon himself (Virgil)
spes tutissima caelis	the safest hope is in heaven
spiritus	spirit; breath
spiritus asper	rough breathing
spiritus lenis	smooth breathing
spiritus rectus	ruling spirit
spiritus vini	alcoholic spirit
spiritus vini vitis	brandy
spiritus vini rectificatus	rectified spirit of wine
splendide mendax	splendidly false (Horace)
spolia optima	the choicest spoils (Livy)
sponte sua	of one's own free will

sportula	a small basket
spetae iniuria formae	an insult to her slighted beauty (Virgil)
Stabat Mater	the mother was standing; hymn concerning the agony of the Virgin Mary at the Crucifixion
stans pede in uno	standing on one foot; with ease (Horace)
stare decisis	to stand by that which was decided; judicial doctrine
stare super antiquas vias	to stand on the old paths
stat fortuna domus virtute	the fortune of the house stands by its virtue
statim	at once
stat magni nomini umbra	he stands in the shadow of a great name
stat nulla diu mortalibus usquam, fortuna titubante, fides	men do not remain loyal for long where Fortune proves unstable
stat promissa fides	the promised faith remains
stat pro ratione voluntas	will stands for reason
status quo	the existing state of things
status quo ante	the situation prevailing before
status quo ante bellum	the situation existing before the war
sta viator, heroem calcas	stop traveler, you stand on a hero's dust
stemma codicum	family tree of manuscripts (for text history)
stet	let it stand

stet fortuna domus	may the good fortune of the house endure
stet pro ratione voluntas	let will stand for reason
stillicidii causa lapidem cavat	dripping water hollows out a stone
stratum super stratum	layer upon layer
strenua inertia	energetic idleness (Horace)
stricto sensu	in a strict sense
strictum ius	strict law
studiis et rebus honestis	by honorable pursuits and studies (motto of the University of Vermont)
studium immane loquendi	an insatiable desire for talking (Ovid)
stultorum calami carbones moenia chartae	chalk is the pen of fools, walls their paper
stultum facit fortuna quem vult perdere	whom Fortune would ruin she deprives of good sense
stupor mundi	wonder of the world
sua cuique sunt vitia	everyone has his own vices
sua cuique utilitas	to everything its own use (Tacitus)
sua cuique voluptas	everyone has his own pleasures
sua munera mittit cum hamo	he sends the gift with a hook attached
sua sponte	of one's self; without prompting
suave mari magno	how pleasant on the great sea (Lucretius)
sunviter et fortiter	gently and firmly

suaviter in modo, fortiter in re	gentle in manner, resolute in action
sub audi	hear under; read between the lines
sub colore iuris	under color of law
sub conditione	upon the condition
sub cruce candida	under the pure white Cross
sub cruce salus	salvation under the Cross
sub dio	under the open sky
subdola cum ridet placidi pellacia ponti	the calm sea shows her false alluring smile
sub ferula	under the rod
sub finem	towards the end
sub hoc signo vinces	under this sign you will conquer
subinde	frequently
sub initio	at the beginning
sub Iove	under Jupiter
sub Iove frigido	under cold Jupiter
sub judice	under a judge; a case not yet decided
sublata causa, tollitur effectus	when the cause is removed, the effect is removed
sublimi feriam sidera vertice	with my head held up, I shall strike the stars (Horace)
sub modo	under a qualification; subject to a condition
sub nomine	under a name; under an alternative title
sub poena	under penalty; writ demanding performance

sub poena ad testificandum	writ compelling one to testify in court
sub poena duce tecum	writ compelling witness to testify in court and to bring evidence
sub quandum aeternitatis	under a certain form of eternity
sub quocunque titulo	under whatever title
sub rosa	under the rose; in secret, in confidence
sub sigillo	under the seal
sub silentio	under silence; silently and in confidence
sub specie	under the appearance of
sub specie aeternitatis	under the aspect of eternity
sub spe rati	in the hope of a decision
sub tegmine fagi	under the cover of the tree (Virgil)
sub verbo	under the word; cross-reference in text
sub vino	under the influence of wine
sub voce	under that heading, under that category
succedaneum	a substitute; one acting in another's place
successore novo vincitur omnis amor	all love is vanquished by a succeeding love (Ovid)
successum fortuna, experientiam laus sequitur	good fortune follows success, praise follows effort (Varro)
sufficit	it is sufficient
suggestio falsi	misrepresentation to conceal the truth

sui cuique fingunt fortunam	one's character creates one's fate
sui generis	of its own kind, in a class by itself, unique
sui juris	capable of assuming legal responsibility
suis stat viribus	he stands on his own strength
sumat	let one take
sumat talem	take one such
sumendum	let it be taken
summa	summary treatise covering the entire subject
summa cum laude	with highest praise; with highest distinction
summa petit livor	it is the highest things that envy seeks (Ovid)
summa potestas	supreme power; the rule of the state
summa sedes non capit duos	the highest seat does not hold two
summa summarum	the sum of all things
summo studio	with the greatest zeal (Cicero)
summum bonum	the highest good
summum genus	the most inclusive classification
summum jus	the highest law
summum jus summa injuria	extreme law, extreme injustice (Cicero)
summum nec metuas diem nec optes	neither fear nor wish for your last day
sumptibus publicis	at public expense

sumptus censum ne superet	let not your spending exceed your income
sunt bona, sunt quaedam mediocria, sunt mala plura	some things are good, some are mediocre, but most are bad (Martial)
sunt lacrimae rerum	there are tears for things; sadness in life is inevitable
sunt lacrimae rerum, et mentem mortalia tangunt	there are tears for sufferings in life and mortal woes touch the heart (Virgil)
suo iure	by his or her own right
suo loco	in its proper place
suo Marte	by one's assertion
suo motu	by one's own motion; spontaneously
suo nomine	in one's own name
suo periculo	at one's own danger
suo tempore	at one's own time; at its own time
super flumina Babylonia	by the rivers of Babylon (Psalm 137)
superstitione tollenda religio non tollitur	religion is not destroyed by eliminating superstition (Cicero)
suppressio veri	willful misrepresentation to suppress the truth
suppressio veri suggestio falsi	suppression of the truth is the suggestion of falsehood
supra	above (in text)
supra vires	beyond one's powers
supremum vale	farewell for the last time
surgit amari aliquid	something bitter rises (Lucretius)

sursum	upwards (motto of Arizona University)
Sursum Corda	lift up your hearts (hymn of the Mass)
sursum reddere	to render upwards; to surrender
suspendatur per collum	let him be hanged by the neck
suspendens omnia naso	turning up the nose at everything (Horace)
suspensio per collum	hanging by the neck
suspiria de profundis	sighs from the depths
sutor, ne supra crepidam	cobbler, stick to your last
suum cuique	to each his own
suu cuique mos	everyone has his own custom

T

tabula rasa	a blank tablet (John Locke)
tace	be silent
tacent, satis laudant	they are silent, they praise enough (Terence)
tacet	it is silent; be silent
tacitans melior mulier semper quam loquens	a woman is better seen than heard
tacite	silently
tacitum vivit sub pectore vulnus	the silent wound lives deep within the breast (Virgil)
taedium vitae	weariness of life
tales	such; such men
talis qualis	such as it is
tam facti quam animi	as much in deed as in intention
tam Marte quam Minerva	as much by Mars as by Minerva
tamquam alter idem	as if a second self (Cicero)
tandem fit surculus arbor	a seedling soon becomes a tree
tangere ulcus	to touch a sore spot
tantae molis erat	so vast a work it was (Virgil)
tantaene animis caelestibus irae?	can such great anger dwell in heavenly minds? (Virgil)

tantas componere lites	to settle such great disputes
Tantum Ergo	so great, therefore (hymn of the Eucharist)
tantum quantum	just as much as
tantum religio potuit suadere malorum	how potent is religion in persuading one to evil actions (Lucretius)
tantus amor scribendi	such a passion for writing (Horace)
tarde venientibus ossa	for latecomers, the bones
Te adoramus	we adore Thee
tecum vivere amem, tecum obeam libens	I wish to love, live, and die with thee (Horace)
Te Deum, laudamus	we praise Thee, God; hymn of thanksgiving
te hominem esse memento	remember that you are a man
Te Igitur	Thee therefore (part of the Eucharist)
te judice	you being the judge
telum imbelle sine ictu	a feeble weapon without the thrust (Virgil)
tempora acta	times past
tempora mutantur nos et mutaur in illis	times change and we change with them
tempora parendum	one must move with the times
tempora si fuerint nubila, solus eris	at times if clouds appear, you will be alone (Ovid)
tempori parendum	one must yield to the times
temporibus inserviendum	one must pay attention to the times
temporis ars medicina fere est	time is the best means of healing (Ovid)

tempus	time
tempus abire tibi est	it is time for you to depart (Horace)
tempus anima rei	time is the soul of things
tempus edax rerum	times devours all things
tempus fugit	time flies
tempus in ultimum	to the last extremity
tempus ludendi	a time for playing
tempus omnia revelat	time reveals all things
tempus rerum imperator	time is sovereign over all things
tenax et fidelis	steadfast and faithful
tenax propositi	tenacious of purpose
tenere lupum auribus	to hold a wolf by the ears
te nosce	know thyself
tentanda via est	the way must be tried
tere bene	rub well
teres atque rotundus	polished and round; well-rounded
ter in die	three times a day
ter in nocte	three times a night
terminus ad quem	the latest possible date for an event
terminus ante quem	established time before event occurred
terminus a quo	the earliest possible starting point
terminus post quem	established time after an event occurred
ter quaterque beatus	three and four times blessed (Virgil)
terra	earth; soil

terra culta	cultivated landterrae filiusson of earth; satirical orator at Oxford
terra es, terram ibis	you are dust, you will return to dust
terra firma	dry land
terra incognita	unknown realm, unexplored region
terras irradient	let them illuminate the lands (motto of Amherst College)
Tersanctus	three times holy; the Trisagion
tertium	third
tertium non datur	the third term not being given
tertium quid	a third something; something intermediate or unknown
tertius gaudens	a third party who profits from a dispute between two other parties
testis unus, testis nullus	one witness, (the same as) no witness
tetigisti acu	you have touched it with a needle (Plautus)
thesaurus inventus	a treasure trove
tibi seris, tibi metis	you sow for yourself, you reap for yourself (Cicero)
time Deum, cole regem	fear God, honor the king
timeo Danaos et dona ferentes	I fear the Greeks even when bearing gifts (Virgil)
timeo hominem unius libri	I fear the man of one book (Thomas Aquinas)

timet pudorem	he fears shame
timor mortis morte peior	the fear of death is worse than death
timor primus in orbe deos fecit	fear was the first creator of the gods in the world (Statius)
toga candida	the white toga worn by Roman candidates
toga praetexta	toga with purple border worn by magistrates
togata	a free woman; prostitute (because she wore the toga rather than the upper-class stola)
toga virilis	adult toga assumed by boys at age fourteen
tot homines quot sententiae	so many men, so many opinions (Terence)
totidem verbis	in so many words
toties quoties	on each occasion
totis viribus	with all one's might
toto caelo	by the entire heavens; worlds apart
totum	the whole
totum divisum	a unit incapable of being divided
totum in eo est	it all depends on this
totus in toto, et totus in qualibet parte	complete as a whole and complete in every part
totus teres atque rotundus	polished and well-rounded in all things
tractent fabrilia fabri	let craftsmen perform only their craft
trahit sua quemque voluptas	his own delight draws each man (Virgil)

transeat in exemplum	let it serve as an example
transit in rem judicatum	it passes into a matter already judged
Treuga Dei	the Truce of God (also **Treva Dei**)
tria iuncta in uno	three joined in one (motto of Order of Bath)
tristis eris si solus eris	you will be sad if you remain alone (Ovid)
trium litterarum homo	a man of three letters; a thief
triumpho morte tam vita	I triumph in death, as in life
trivium	grammar, rhetoric and logic
Troia fuit	Troy was (and will be no more)
Tros Tyriusque mihi nullo dicrimine agentur	Trojan and Tyrian shall be treated by me with no discrimination (Virgil)
truditur dies die	one day is pushed on to another (Horace)
tu, Domine, gloria mea	thou, O Lord, art my glory
tuebor	I shall defend (the Great Seal of Michigan)
tu ne cede malis sed contra audentior ito	yield not to misfortunes, but advance more boldly against them
tu nihil invita dices faciesve Minerva	you will say or do nothing when Minerva is unwilling (Horace)
tu quoque	and you also (used to indict the accuser in a court of law)
tutius erratur ex parte mitiore	it is safer to err on the gentler side
tutor et ultor	protector and avenger

U

uberrima fides	the highest degree of trust
ubi amici, ibi opes	where there are friends, there is wealth
ubi bene, ibi patria	where I prosper, there is my country
ubi est autem dignitas nisi ubi honestas?	what is dignity without honesty?
ubi homines sunt, modi sunt	where there are men, there are manners
ubi innocens damnatur, pars patriae exsulat	when an innocent man is convicted, part of his country is exiled
ubi ius incertum, ibi ius nulum	where the law is uncertain, there is no law
ubi lapsus? quid feci?	where have I fallen? what have I done?
ubi libertns ibi patria	where there is freedom, there is my country
ubi mel ibi apes	where there is honey, there will be bees
ubique	everywhere
ubique patriam reminisci	everywhere to remember our country
ubi solitudinem faciunt pacem appellant	where they create desolation, they call it peace (Tacitus)

ubi sunt qui ante nos fuerunt?	where are those who lived before us? (often shortened to **ubi sunt?**)
ubi supra	where above
ubi vinci necesse est, expedit cedere	where defeat is inevitable, it is wisest to yield
ultima forsan	perhaps the last
ultima praescripta	the last ordered
ultima ratio	the final argument
ultima ratio regum	the final argument of kings (war)
ultima Thule	the farthest point accessible (Virgil)
ultimo	in the last month
ultimum vale	farewell for the last time
ultimus heres	the last heir
ultimus regum	the last of the kings
ultimus Romanorum	the last of the Romans
ultra	beyond; more than
ultra licitum	beyond that which is allowed
ultra posse nemo obligatur	no one is bound to do more than he can
ultra valorem	beyond the value
ultra vires	outside one's jurisdiction; beyond the scope
umbra	shadow; shade
una et eadem persona	one and the same person
una salus victis nullam sperare salutem	the one safety for the conquered is to abandon hope for salvation (Virgil)

una si qua placet, culta puella sat est
admired by one man, a girl is adorned (Propertius)

una voce
with one voice; unanimously

unguibus et rostro
with claws and beak; with all one's might

unguis in ulcere
a claw in the wound

uni aequus virtuti, atque eius amicis
friendly to virtue alone and to the friends of virtue (Horace)

unica virtus necessaria
virtue is the only thing necessary

uni cuique dedit vitium natura creato
Nature has conferred some vice on each created thing (Propertius)

Unitas Fratrum
unity of brethren (the Moravian Church)

unius dementia dementes efficit multos
the madness of one drives man mad

uno animo
with one mind

uno ictu
at one blow

uno saltu
in one leap

unus vir nullus vir
one man (is the same as) no man

urbem latericiam invenit, marmoream reliquit
he found the city brick and left it marble (Suetonius on Julius Caesar)

urbi et orbi
to the city (Rome) and to the world

urbs in horto
a city in a garden (motto of Chicago)

urceus
earthenware pitcher

usque
even to

usque ad aras	even to the altars
usque ad nauseam	even to the point of sickness
usus est optimus magister	experience is the best teacher
usus est tyrannus	custom is a tyrant
usus loquendi	usage to speak
usus promptos facit	use makes men ready
usus te plura docebit	experience will teach you many things
ut ameris, amabilis esto	that you may be loved, show love (Ovid)
ut apes geometriam	as bees (practice) geometry
utcumque placuerint Deo	as it shall please God
ut dictum	as directed
ut fata trahunt	as the Fates drag
ut homo est, ita morem geras	as a man is, so must you humor him (Terence)
utile dulci	the useful with the agreeable
utinam noster esset	would that he were ours
utinam tam facile vera invenire possem quam falsa convincere	I only wish I could discover truth as easily as I expose falsehood (Cicero)
ut infra	see below (in a text)
uti non abuti	to use, not to abuse
uti possidetis	as you possess it (you may keep it)
ut mos est	as is the custom (Juvenal)
ut pictura poesis	poetry is like a painting (Horace)
ut pignus amicitiae	as a pledge of friendship
ut prosim	that I may be of use

ut quocunque paratus	prepared on every side
utrum horum mavis accipe	take whichever you prefer
ut saepe summa ingenia in occulto latent	the greatest talents are often shrouded in obscurity
ut supra	see above (in a text)

V

vacuo — in a vacuum

vacuus cantat coranm latrone viator — the traveler with an empty purse sings before the robber

vade in pace — go in peace

vade mecum — go with me; a guidebook, a reference book

vade retro me, Satana — get behind me, Satan (Gospel of Mark)

vadonium mortuum — a mortgage

vae soli — woe to the solitary person

vae victis — woe to the conquered

vagitus — the first cry of a newborn child

vale — farewell

valeat quantum valere potest — let it stand for what it is worth

valet ancora virtus — virtue serves as an anchor

valete ac plaudite — farewell and applaud

vanitas vanitatum, omnis vanitas — vanity of vanities, all is vanity (Ecclesiastes)

vani timoris iusta excusatio non est — empty fear is not a legitimate excuse

varia lectio — a variant rendering of a text

variatim — variously, in various ways

variorum	of various persons; a literary text with comments from other writers or critics
variorum notae	notes of various commentators
varium et mutabile semper femina	woman is ever fickle and changeable (Virgil)
vectigalia nervi sunt rei publicae	revenues are the sinews of the state (Cicero)
vel caeco apparent	it would be apparent even to a blind man
velis et remis	with sails and oars; a total effort
vel prece vel pretio	either with prayer or with price
velut aegri somnia	like a sick man's dream (Horace)
venalis populus venalis curia patrum	both the people and the senators can be bribed
vendidit hic nuro patriam	he sold his country for gold
venenum in auro bibitur	poison is drunk from a golden cup
venia necessitati datur	indulgence is granted to necessity
veni, Creator Spiritus	come Creator Spirit (Book of Common Prayer)
venienti occurrite morbo	meet the approaching disease
venire	to come; the process of selection of jurors
venire facias	make to come; writ summoning the jurors

Venite	Come (Psalm 95) (sung at Morning Prayer)
venit summa dies et ineluctabile tempus	the last day has come and the inevitable hour is here (Virgil)
veni, vidi, vici	I came, I saw, I conquered (Julius Caesar)
ventis secundis	with favorable winds
ventre nihil novi frugalis	nothing is more easily satisfied than the stomach (Juvenal)
vera causa	a true cause
vera incessu patuit dea	by her walk the true goddess was revealed (Virgil)
verbatim	word for word; exactly as quoted
verbatim et litteratim	word for word and letter for letter
verba volant, scripta manent	spoken words fly away, written words remain
verbera, sed audi	strike, but hear me
Verbi Dei Minister	Preacher of the Word of God
verbis ad verbera	from words to blows
verbum sat sapienti est	a word is enough for a wise man
verbum satis est	a word is enough
veritas	truth (motto of Harvard)
veritas entis	truth of being
veritas nunquam perit	truth never dies
veritas odium parit	truth engenders hatred (Terence)
veritas omnia vincit	truth conquers all things

veritas praevalebit	truth will prevail
veritas temporis filia	truth is the daughter of time
veritas victrix	truth the conqueror
veritas vos liberabit	the truth shall make you free (motto of Johns Hopkins University)
veritas vincit	truth conquers
veritatem dies aperit	time reveals the truth
veritatis simplex oratio est	the language of truth is simple (Seneca)
verso	the left-hand page of a book
verte	turn the page
vestigia	footprints; traces or remains
vestigia morientis libertatis	the footprints of a dying liberty
vestigia nulla retrorsum	no footsteps backwards (Horace)
vestigia terrent	the footprints frighten me (Horace)
veteris vestigia flammae	remnants of an ancient flame (Virgil)
via amicabili	in a friendly way
Via Crucis	the Way of the Cross, stations of the Cross
via crucis, via lucis	the way of the Cross is the way of light
Via Dolorosa	the road of sadness (the road Christ followed on the way to the Crucifixion)
Via Lactea	the Milky Way
via media	middle course between two extremes

via militaris	a military road
via trita, vin tuta	the beaten path is the safe path
viaticum	the Eucharist administered to dying person
vice versa	conversely; the positions being reversed
vicisti, Galilaee	thou hast conquered, O Man of Galilee
victi vicimus	conquered, we conquer
victis honor	honor to the conquered
victoria concordia crescit	victory is increased by concord
victoria fortunae sapientia	wisdom is the victor over fortune (Juvenal)
victor ludorum	the winner of athletic contests
vide	see
vide ante	see before
vide et crede	see and believe
vide infra	see below
vide post	see after
vide supra	see above
vide ut infra	see as below
vide ut supra	see as above
videlicet (viz.)	one may see; that is to say
video barbam et pallium, philosophum nondum video	I see the beard and the cloak, I have yet to see the philosopher
video meliora proboque, deteriora sequor	I see the better way and approve it, but I follow the worse way (Ovid)
videtur	it appears; it seems

229

vidit et erubuit lympha pudica Deum — the modest water saw God and blushed

vi et armis — by force of arms

vigilandum est semper; multae insidiae sunt bonis — one must always be on one's guard; there are many snares for the good

vigilantibus — to the watchful

vigilante et ora — watch and pray

vilius argentum est auro, virtutibus aurum — silver is worth less than gold, gold is worth less than virtue (Horace)

vincam aut moriar — I will conquer or die

vincere scis, Hannibal, victoria uti nescis — you know how to vanquish Hannibal, but you do not know how to enjoy victory (Livy)

vincet amor patriae laudumque immensa cupido — love of country conquers the boundless desire for glory (Virgil)

vincit omnia veritas — truth conquers all things

vincit qui patitur — he who prevails is patient

vincit qui se vincit — he conquers who conquers himself (Publius Syrus)

vincit veritas — truth conquers

vinculum matrimonii — the bond of marriage

vindex injuriae — the avenger of wrong

vino tortus et ira — tortured by wine and anger (Horace)

vir bonus dicendi peritus — a good man skilled in the art of speaking

vires acquirit eundo — it gains strength by going (Virgil)

virescit vulnere virtus — virtue flourished from a wound

viret in aeternum	it flourishes forever
vir et uxor	husband and wife
Virgilium vidi tantum	I have only seen Virgil (Ovid)
virginibus puerisque canto	I sing for maidens and boys (Virgil)
Virgo	the Virgin
Virgo Sapientissima	Virgin Most Wise
Virgo Sponsa Dei	Virgin Bride of the Lord
viribus totis	with all one's strength
viribus unitis	with united strength
viri infelicis procul amici	friends stay away from the unfortunate man
virorum volitare per ora	to fly through the mouths of men (Ennius)
vir sapit qui pauca loquitur	the man is wise who talks little
virtus	virtue; manly excellence
virtus ariete fortior	virtue is stronger than a battering ram
virtus est militis decus	virtue is the soldier's glory
virtus est medium vitiorum et utrimque reductum	virtue is the mean between vices, as far from one extreme as from the other (Horace)
virtus in actione consistit	virtue consists of action
virtus in arduis	virtue in difficulties
virtus incendit vires	virtue kindles one's strength
virtus laudatur et alget	virtue is praised and left to freeze
virtus millia scuta	virtue is a thousand shields
virtus nobilitat	virtue ennobles

virtus non stemma	virtue not ancestral stock
virtus post nummos	virtue after wealth (Horace)
virtus probata florescit	virtue flourishes in a trial
virtus requiei nescia sordidae	virtue knowing nothing of base leisure
virtus semper viridis	virtue is always green
virtus sola nobilitat	virtue alone can ennoble
virtus vincit invidium	virtue overcomes envy
virtus vincit omnia	virtue conquers all things
virtute et armis	by courage and arms (motto of Mississippi)
virtute et fide	by virtue and faith
virtute et labore	by virtue and toil
virtute et opere	by virtue and industry
virtute, non astutia	by virtue, not by craft
virtute, non verbis	by virtue, not by words
virtute, non viris	by virtue, not by men
virtute officii	by virtue of office
virtute quies	in virtue there is calm
virtute securus	secure by means of virtue
virtuti nihil obstat et armis	nothing can withstand valor and arms
virtuti non armis fido	I trust in virtue and not in arms
virtutis amore	from love of virtue
virtutis avorum praemium	the reward of the valor of my ancestors
virtutis fortuna comes	fortune is the companion of valor (motto of the Duke of Wellington)
virtuti sis par, dispar fortunis patris	be like your father in courage, unlike him in fortune

vis	force, power, strength (plural **vires**)
vis a fronte	a force in front
vis a tergo	a force from behind
vis comica	a comic force
vis conservatrix	the preservative force (Horace)
vis consilii expers mole ruit sua	force without good sense falls by its own weight (Horace)
vis inertiae	power of inactivity
vis major	a greater force; a superior force
vis medicatrix naturae	the healing power of nature
vis mortua	dead force
vis unita fortior	force is increased by union
vis vitalis	vital force
vita brevis, ars longa	life is short, art is long
vitae summa brevis spem nos vetat inchoare longam	life's short span forbids us to enter on far reaching hopes (Virgil)
vitae via virtus	virtue is the way of life
vitam impendere vero	to devote one's life to truth (Juvenal)
vitam regit fortuna non sapientia	chance, not wisdom, governs life
vita non est vivere sed valere vita est	life is not to live, but life is to be strong (Martial)
vita sine litteris mors est	life without literature is death
vitavi denique culpam, non laudem merui	I have saved myself from blame, but I have not earned praise (Horace)

vitiis nemo sine nascitur	no one is born without faults
vivamus, mea Lesbia, atque amemus	let us live, my Lesbia, and let us love (Catullus)
vivant rex et regina	long live the king and queen
vivas ut possis quando nequis ut velis	live as you can since you cannot live as you wish
vivat	long live
vivat Caesar	long live Caesar
vivat regina	long live the queen
vivat res publica	long live the commonwealth
vivat rex	long live the king
viva voce	with lively, loud voice
vive hodie	live today (Martial)
vive memor leti	live mindful of death (Persius)
vivendi causa	cause of living
vivere commune est, sed non commune mereri	to live is common to all, but to be worthy of living is not
vivere est cogitare	to live is to think (Cicero)
vivere parvo	to live on little
vivere sat vincere	to conquer and to live enough
vive ut vivas	live so that you may live
vive et vale	live and be well
vive, vale	live and farewell (Horace)
vivida vis animi	the living force of the mind

vivite fortes fortiaque adversis opponite pectora rebus	live as brave men, and if fortune is adverse accept its blows with brave hearts (Horace)
vivit post funera virtus	virtue lives after the grave (Tiberius)
vix ea nostra vovo	I can hardly call these things my own
vixere fortes ante Agamemnona	brave men lived before Agamemnon (Horace)
vixit	he or she has lived
volat hora per orbem	time flies through the world
volens et potens	willing and able
volente Deo	God willing
volenti non fit injuria	there can be no injury to one who consents
volo non valeo	I am willing but unable
voluntas habeatur pro facto	the will be taken for the deed
voluptates commendat rarior usus	rare indulgence increases pleasure
voluptates corporis	the sensual pleasures of the body
volventibus annis	with revolving years
vota vita men	my life is devoted
vox	voice
vox angelica	angel's voice; organ stop producing the sound of strings
vox audita perit littera scripta manet	the voice perishes, but written words remain
vox barbara	barbaric voice; a foreign word

vox clamans in deserto	a voice crying in the wilderness (motto of Yale)
vox clamantis in deserto	the voice of one crying in the wilderness (the Gospel of Matthew)
vox clandestina	a secret voice; a whisper
vox et praeterea nihil	a voice and nothing more (Plutarch)
vox faucibus haesit	one's voice stuck in the throat
vox humana	organ stop resembling the human voice
vox populi	the voice of the people; general consensus
vox populi, vox Dei	the voice of the people is the voice of God
vox stellarum	the voice of the stars
vulgare amici nomen, sed rara est fides	the name of friend is common, but true friendship is rare
vulgo	in a common manner
vulgus amicitias utilitate probat	the common herd values friendship for its own usefulness (Ovid)
vulneratus non victus	wounded but not conquered
vultus est index animi	the face is a sign of the soul

APPENDIX 1

Summary of Major Latin Writers

Note: This list includes only the most popular or most influential works by these writers and should not be construed as being comprehensive.

Apuleius
On the God of Socrates
On Plato and His Dogma
Florida (Boquet)
Apologia (Apology)
Metamorphoses (The Golden Ass)

St. Augustine
Confessions
The City of God

Marcus Aurelius
Meditations

Julius Caesar
De Bello Gallico (The Gallic War)
De Bello Civili (The Civil War)

Catullus
Poems

Cicero
Rhetorica
Epistulae

A few major groups include:
   De Senectute (Of Old Age)
   De Amicitia (On Friendship)
   Ad Atticum (Letters to Atticus)
   Ad Familiares (Letters to Friends)
Orationes

Two major groups include:
   De Catiline (Against Catiline)

Philippics (Against Antony)

Ennius   *Annals*

Epictetus   *Moral Discourses*

Horace   *Satires*
                    Satires II
                    Epodes
                    Odes
                    Odes II
                    Ars Poetica
                    Carmen Saeculare
                    Epistles
                    Epistles II

St. Jerome   *The Vulgate*
                    Chronicles

Josephus   *Vita (Autobiography)*
                    Bellum Judaicum (The Jewish War)
                    Jewish Antiquities
                    Against Apion

Juvenal   *Saturae (Satires)*

Lactantius   *Institutiones Diviniae*
                    De Mortibus Persecutorum

Livy   *Ab Urbe Condita (From the Foundation of
                    the City)*

Lucan   *Pharsalia (The Civil War)*

Lucilius   *Sermones (Discourses)*

Lucretius   *De Rerum Natura (On the Nature of Things)*

Martial   *Liber Spectaculorum (Book of Spectacles)*
                    Xenia (Guest Gifts)
                    Apophoreta (Party Favors)
                    Epigrammata (Epigrams

Naevius   *Bellum Punicum (The Punic War)*

Nepos   *De Viris Illustribus*

Ovid   *Amores (Love Poems)*

Heroides *(The Demigoddesses)*
Ars Amatoria *(The Art of Love)*
Remedia Amoris *(The Cure of Love)*
Metamorphoses *(Transformations)*
Tristia *(Sadness)*
Fasti *(Holidays)*
Epistulae Ex Pono *(Letters from the Black Sea)*

Persius Saturae *(Satires)*

Petroinius Cena Trimalchionis *(Trimalchio's Dinner Party)*

Plautus Menaechmi *(The Twin Menaechmi)*
Miles Gloriosus *(The Boastful Soldier)*
Cistellaria *(The Casket)*
Aulularia *(The Pot of Gold)*
Amphitryon
Asinaria *(The Comedy of Asses)*
Stichus
Psedolus
Truculentus
Captivi *(The Captives)*

Pliny the Elder Naturalis Historia *(Natural History)*

Pliny the Younger Panegyric on Trajan
Epistulae *(Letters)*

Plutarch Parallel Lives
Moral Essays

Propertius Elegies

Quintilian Institutio Oratoriae

Sallust Catilina
Jugurtha

Seneca Moral Essays
Octavia
Medea
Phaedra

Statius Thebaid *(Deeds of the Seven Against Thebes)*

Silvae (Forest Books)
Achilleid (The Death of Achilles)

Suetonius

De Viris Illustribus (Illustrious Men)
De Vita Caesarum (Lives of the Caesars)
De Grammaticis (Grammar)
De Rhetoribus (Rhetoric)

Tacitus

Germania
Agricola
Dialogue on Orators
Histories
Annals

Terence

Andria (The Girl from Andros)
Hecyra (Her Husband's Mother)
Heauton Timorumenos (The Self-Tormentor)
The Eunuch
Phormio
Adelphoe (The Brothers)

Tertullian

Treatises

Tibullus

Elegies

Virgil

Eclogues
Georgics
The Aeneid

APPENDIX 2

Summary of Major Greek Writers

Note: This list includes only the most popular or most influential works by these writers and should not be considered a complete listing. The listings for Aeschylus, Sophocles, Euripides, and Aristophanes include all of their extant plays.

Aeschylus	*The Oresteia*
	Agamemnon
	The Choephoroe
	The Eumenides
	Prometheus Bound
	The Persians
	The Seven Against Thebes
	The Suppliants
Aesop	*Fables*
Alcaeus	*Poems*
Apollonius of Rhodes	*Argonautica*
Aristophanes	*Lysistrata*
	The Birds
	The Clouds
	The Frogs
	The Wasps
	Peace
	Thesmorphoriazusae
	Ecclesiazusae
	The Acharnians
	The Knights
	Plutus

Aristotle
Logic
Physics
Metaphysics
On Animals
Nicomachean Ethics
Politics
Rhetoric
Poetics

Callimachus
Hymns
Epigrams

Demosthenes
Orationes
The Philippics

Euripides
Medea
Electra
Alcestis
Hippolytus
Andromache
The Trojan Woman
The Heracleidae
The Suppliants
Hecuba
Rhesus
Heracles
Ion
Helena
Iphigenia in Tauris
The Phoenician Women
Orestes
The Bacchae
Iphigenia at Aulis
The Cyclops

Herodotus
History of the Persian Wars

Hesiod
Works and Days
Theogony

Homer
The Illiad
The Odyssey

Isocrates
Panegyricus

Loginus	*On the Sublime*
Lysias	*Orationes* *Against Eratosthenes*
Menander	*The Shearing of Glycera* *The Girl from Samos* *The Arbitration* *Dyskolos*
Pindar	*Olympian Odes* *Pythian Odes*
Plato	*Apology* *Crito* *Phaedo* *Euthyphro* *Meno* *Symposium* *Protagoras* *Gorgias* *The Republic* *The Statesmen*
Plotinus	*The Enneads*
Polybius	*The History*
Sappho	*Love Poems*

Sophocles	The Theban Plays
	    Oedipus Rex
	    Oedipus at Colonus
	    Antigone
	Ajax
	Electra
	The Trachiniae
	Philoctetes

Theocritus	*The Idylls*
Thucydides	*History of the Peloponnesian Wars*
Xenophon	*Anabasis* *Hellenica*

APPENDIX 3

Mottoes of Selected States

Alabama:
**udemus jura nostra
defendere**

we dare to defend our
rights

Arizona:
ditat Deus

God enriches

Arkansas:
regnat populus

the people rule

Colorado:
nil sine numine

nothing without divine
will

Connecticut:
qui transtulit sustinet

He who transplanted,
sustains

District of Columbia:
iustitia omnibus

justice for all

Kansas:
ad astra per aspera

to the stars through
difficulties

Maine:
dirigo

I direct

Massachusetts:
**ense petit placidam sub
libertate quietam**

with the sword she seeks
calm repose under
liberty

Michigan:
**si quaëris peninsulam
amoenam, circumspice**

if you seek a beautiful
peninsula, look around

Mississippi:
virtute et armis   by valor and arms

Missouri:
salus populi suprema   let the welfare of the
  lex esto   people be the supreme
                                          law

New Mexico:
crescit eundo   it grows as it goes

New York:
excelsior   even higher

North Carolina:
esse quam videri   to be rather than to seem

Oklahoma:
labor omnia vincit   work conquers all things

Oregon:
alias volat propriis   she flies with her own
                                          wings

South Carolina:
1. aimis opibusque parati   prepared in spirits and
                                          resources
2. dum spiro spero   while I breathe, I hope

Virginia:
sic semper tyrannis   thus ever to tyrants

West Virginia:
montani semper liberi   mountaineers are always
                                          free men

Wyoming:
cedant arma togae   let arms yield to the toga

Great Seal of U.S.:
1. novus ordo seclorum   a new order of the ages
2. annuit coeptis   He has smiled on our
                                          undertaking
3. e pluribus unum   one out of many

APPENDIX 4

150 Most Common Latin Phrases

ab imo pectore	from the bottom of the heart
ab ovo usuque ad mala	from the egg to the apples (beginning to end)
ab urbe condita (A.U.C.)	from the foundation of the city (753 B.C.)
absit omen	may the omen be absent, God forbid
a capite ad calcem	from head to heel, completely
ad hominem	personal or related to the individual
ad infinitum	without an end, to infinity
ad libitum	at pleasure or extemporaneously
ad nausem	to the point of sickness or disgust
ad valorem	according to value
a fortiori	with an even stronger reason
alter ego	one's second self, close friend
alter idem	another thing precisely similar
amicus curiae	friend of the court

annus mirabilis	wonderful year, remarkable year
a posteriori	inductive reasoning, from effect to cause
a priori	deductive reasoning, from cause to effect
arbiter elgantiae	dictator of fashion, judge of fine tastes
ars longa, vita brevis	art is long, life is short
bene vobis	may you prosper and be healthy
bona fide	in good faith, genuine, legitimate
carpe diem	seize the day, enjoy the moment
casus belli	reason for war, grounds for a dispute
caveat emptor	let the buyer beware
caveat vendor	let the seller beware
ceteris paribus	other things being equal
cogito, ergo sum	I think, therefore I am
corpus delicti	the facts proving a crime
compos mentis	in a sound state of mind
decessit sine prole (D.S.P.)	died without any children
de facto	existing by fact, not by right
de jure	existing by lawful right
Deo optimo maximo (D.O.M.)	for God, the best and greatest
Deo volente	God willing
de profundis	from the depths, out of despair
desideratum	a thing much desired or needed

deus ex machina	god from a machine
dramatis personae	list of characters in a play
ecce homo	behold the man (Christ)
et alia (et al.)	and other things
et cetera (etc.)	and the rest
et hoc genus omne	and all others of that sort
et sequentes (et seq.)	and the following
ex cathedra	from the seat, position of authority
exempli gratia (e.g.)	for example
ex gratia	performed as an act of grace
ex libris	from the library of
ex officio	by virtue of one's office
ex parte	from one side only, partisan
ex post facto	after the fact
ex tempore	spontaneously, without preparation
facta non verba	deeds not words, action is required
factotum	one who does everything
festina lente	make haste slowly
fidei defensor	defender of the faith
fidus Achates	faithful companion
flagrante delicto	in the heat of the crime
habeas corpus	writ requiring presentation of the person before a judge
horribile dictu	horrible to relate
ibidem (ibid.)	the same text
imprimatur	official sanction for publication of a text

in excelsis	in the highest, to the greatest measure
in extenso	in its entirety, completely
in extremis	at the point of death
infra dignitatem	beneath one's dignity
in hoc signo	by this sign (the Cross)
in loco citato (loc. cit.)	occurring in the place cited
in medias res	in the middle of things
in posse	as a possibility, potential action
in principio	in the beginning
in situ	in the original place
inter alia	among other things
intra vires	within one's authority
in vino veritas	in wine, there is truth
ipse dixit	he himself said it
ipso facto	by the fact itself
jacta alea est	the die is cast (Julius Caesar)
jus gentium	international law among nations
lacuna	gap, blank space, missing part
laesa majestas	the crime of high treason
lex talionis	the law of retribution
lite pendente	while the lawsuit is pending
locus classicus	standard source of an idea
lusus natura	freak of nature, unusual occurrence
magnum opus	most important work of writer or artist
mare nostrum	our sea (the Mediterranean)

memento mori	reminder of death
mirabile dictu	wonderful to say
modus operandi	method of operation
modus vivendi	mode of living together
ne plus ultra	nothing more beyond, highest point
nihil obstat	nothing hinders, nothing withstanding
nolle prosequi	prosecutor does not wish to continue
nolo contendere	I do not wish to contend a defense
non placet	it does not please
non sequitur	it does not follow
nota bene	note well
obiter dictum	incidental or passing remark
omnia vincit amor	love conquers all things
opere citato (op. cit)	occurring in the work cited
O tempora, O mores	O the times, O the manners
pari passu	with equal pace, side by side
pax vobiscum	peace be with you
peccavi	I have sinned, I was wrong
persona grata	an acceptable person (diplomat)
persona non grata	an unacceptable person (diplomat)
petitio principii	begging the question (logic)
post hoc, ergo propter hoc	after this, therefore because of this

prima facie	at first glance, at first sight
primus inter pares	first or foremost among equals
pro tempore	temporary, for the moment
quantum libet	as much as you please
quantum meruit	as much as was deserved
quid pro quo	something for something, this for that
quod erat demonstrandum (Q.E.D.)	that which was to be proved
quod erat faciendum (Q.E.F.)	that which was to be done
quod vide (q.v.)	for which to see, refer to
quo vadis?	where are you going?
rara avis	rare bird, an unusual person
ratio decidendi	the essentials of judgment
recto	the right-hand page of a book
requiescat in pace (R.I.P.)	may he or she rest in peace
res ipsa loquitor	the thing speaks for itself
res judicata	the things have been judged
scilicet	it is permitted to know
semper fidelis	always faithful (Marine Corp)
semper paratus	always prepared (Coast Guard)
sic passim	thus throughout (the text)
sic transit gloria mundi	thus passes the glory of the world

sine qua non	fundamental cause, necessary precondition
status quo ante	the situation prevailing before
sub judice	under a judge, case not yet decided
sub poena	under penalty, writ demanding performance
sub rosa	under the rose, in secret, in confidence
sub voce	under that heading, under that category
sui generis	unique, in a class by itself
sui juris	capable of assuming legal responsibility
terminus ad quem	the latest possible date for an event
terminus a quo	the earliest possible starting point
terra incognita	unknown realm, unexplored region
ultima thule	the furthest point accessible
ultra vires	outside one's jurisdiction
ut infra	see below (in a text)
ut supra	see above (in a text)
vade mecum	come with me, a reference book
verbatim	word for word, exactly as quoted
verso	the left-hand page of a book
videlicet	one may see, that is to say

Fifty Most Common Latin Quotations

ad praesens ova cras pullis sunt meliora
eggs today are better than chickens tomorrow

a fronte praeciptium a tergo lupi
a precipice in front and wolves behind

acta est fabula (*Augustus*)
the act is completed

aequam servare mentem (*Horace*)
to preserve a calm mind

albo (nigro) lapillo notare diem
to mark the day with a white (black) stone

animal bipes implume (*Plato*)
a two-legged animal without feathers

arbiter elegantiae (*Petronius*)
arbiter of elegance

arma virumque cano (*Virgil*)
of arms and the man I sing

ars gratia artis (*MGM motto*)
art for art's sake

auro quaeque ianua panditur
a golden key opens any door

aut disce aut discede (*Oxford*)
either learn or leave

ave Caesar, morituri te salutant
Hail Caesar, those of us who are about to die salute you

de gustibus non est disputandum	there is no disputing about tastes
delenda est Carthago (*Cato the Elder*)	Carthage must be destroyed
de morruis nihil nisi bonum	(say) nothing but good about the dead
docendo discimus (quae nocent docent)	we learn by teaching
donec eris felix, multos numerabis amicos (*Ovid*)	as long as you are fortunate, you will have many friends
dulce est descipere in loco (*Horace*)	it is sweet to relax at times
dum vivimus, viviamus (cf. carpe diem)	while we live, let us live
facilis descensus Averno (*Virgil*)	the descent to hell is easy
felix qui nihil debet	happy is he who owes nothing
fortuna favet fortibus (*Terence*)	fortune favors the strong
homo doctus in se semper divitias habet	a learned man always has wealth within himself
incidis in Scyllam cupiens vitare Charybdim	you fall into Scylla wishing to avoid Charybdis
lupus est homo homini (*Plautus*)	man is wolf to man
magni nominis umbra (cf. epigone)	under the shadow of a great name
medio tutissimus ibis (ne quid nimis) (*Ovid*)	you will go safest in the middle
nam et ipsa scientia potestas est (*Bacon*)	for knowledge is itself power

naturam expelles furca tamen usque recurret — you may drive nature out with a pitchfork but it will still return

nil novi sub sole (*Ecclesiastes*) — there is nothing new under the sun

non semper ea sunt quae videntur (*Phaedrus*) — things are never what they seem

non semper erit aetas — it will not always be summer

nosce te ipsum — know thyself

oleum perdisti — you have lost oil

omnia mutantur nos et mutamur in illis — all things change and we change with them

panem et circenses (*Juvenal*) — bread and circuses

paupertas omnium artium repertrix — poverty is the inventor of all arts

post hoc, ergo propter hoc — after this, therefore because of this

quandoque bonus dormitat Homerus (*Horace*) — sometimes even good Homer sleeps

radix omnium malorum est cupiditas — the desire for money is the root of all evil

respice, adspice, prospice — look to the past, look to the present, look to the future

sic transit gloria mundi (*Thomas à Kempis*) — thus passes the glory of the world

sit non doctissima coniux (*Martial*) — may your wife not be very learned

sumptus censum ne superet (*Martial*) — let not your spending exceed your income

temporis ars medicina fere est (*Ovid*) — time is the best means of healing

tempus edax rerum
  (Ovid)

time devours all things

**time Danaos et dona
  ferentes** *(Virgil)*

I fear the Greeks even
  when bearing gifts

**varium et mutabile
  semper femina** *(Virgil)*

woman is fickle and
  changeable